CW00521701

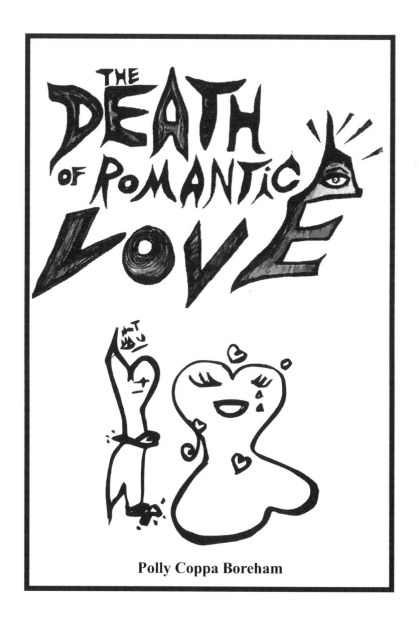

THE DEATH OF ROMANTIC LOVE

Polly Coppa Boreham

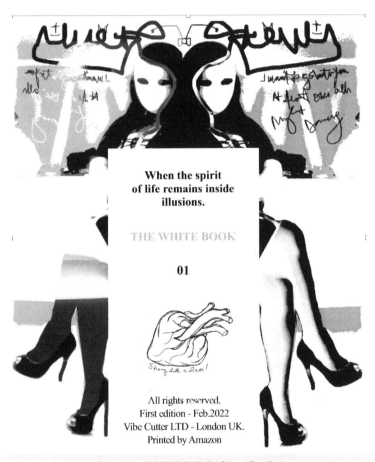

**When the spirit
of life remains inside
illusions.**

THE WHITE BOOK

01

All rights reserved.
First edition - Feb.2022
Vibe Cutter LTD - London UK.
Printed by Amazon

Email for any enquiries: contact@vibecutter.com
For DJ sets - https://www.mixcloud.com/VibeCutter

<u>NAMES WERE CHANGED TO PROTECT THE INNOCENTS.</u>

Look out for this symbol
"Name of the song" (by Name of the Artist).

Please, add the playlist from Spotify using QR:

Other QR codes might be provided along this book, to access apps or
websites, linked to this art work, such as Vimeo, Mixcloud, Instagram,
Opensea, Soundcloud and <u>vibecutter.com</u>

WELCOME.

"Yulunga" Dead Can Dance.

WHERE IS NORTH FROM HERE?

"Sufi Spin" Lemurian & Discoshaman.

Introduction and facts about this book

My quiet voice manifested,
In the hit of the frustration.
Rage blinds us all.
Taking place in ink over the paper,
All the bleeding words of cold kills in riddles,
To stop the pain, in a try to gives us a laugh.

1) In Chaos we Flourish! Almost like an exercise to diminish the ego and to be able to skip the natural fatigue.
The Death of Romantic Love was documented, infused by tales of the joy of illusions. Here I am trying to organise my manuscripts like studies of how the mind behaves in predictable crisis. It's a lighter version of poetry and free writing of the complex journey between ego, self-love, rejection, and illusions.

2) In this book, the presented photos and sketches were also made infused with the universe of my American friend, Cindy.
As the storyteller, I put myself in a modified image of my own, like an actress playing the role of Cindy.
Cindy's physical appearance is exactly the same as mine in real life, not a millimetre taller. Therefor when you see the images here, you're not seeing me, you're seeing Cindy. Together we laugh about our own dramas to blame, since we behaved badly but took the shame. At the end of the day, the truth is whatever you want to be true.

Why this disassociation? Why merge different stories?

3) Over the last 7 years I've made a series of photos, where I've documented intimate moments of the personal love of a model.
Ridiculous, real, emotional, soul-breaking and also funny.

I used a domestic scenario to record the journey of the model in discovering his own self values and identity.

9

There was no bodily interaction linked to this work, which on my part, was journalistic, and for him it was fun. As I was about to finish the book, the model changed his mind, and the images were not authorised to be part of this work.

The images made would not be related to the stories. My idea was to use the discrepancies with images and words, to drive attention to the incompatibility of feelings, that exists in a romantic love relationship. Offering dissonance of image and stories, it is an attempt to illustrate the realm lived by so many couples that have a completely distorted idea of the very reality of their relationship. While one sees darkness the other is saying everything is absolutely fine!

The model does not agree with the idea behind the dissociation of image and text. This was due to a conflict of emotional content associated with the name of the book.

His idea was something more sexual niche, which was directly related to the idea of his personal fun. In the case of those unpublished photos, the focus was only for the sake of being sexualised. The model saw the situation as an expansion of the very expression of sexuality in a very casual and light way. His version is interesting and I am still open to invest some energy to co-create another book more focused on his point of view.

Therefore, at some point in the future we might have a sequel or a much darker second version of this book.

4) Here I recount a personal and group journey where all factors count in the discontinuation of disillusionment, but also I hope to give reason to justify the importance of personal illusions, as energy generators for life-changing actions.

It's a study using the wording of songs and dramatic psychological conversations to observe life as it happens.

Evolving over disposable dramas. Acting upon still life taking illusions is not like a passive escapism but more like something to aim for.

My goal is to be a better person to achieve whatever I desire. Burned out my sorrows, in my emotional management path where everybody hurts and everybody laughs. The most beautiful love, manifests itself from uncomfortable truths. Self-love.

As a couple, upgrading the unachieved forever, as in romantic lovers, to a possible forever, as respectable friends. A contract seal, almost like an imaginary shaken hands agreement, welcoming the new sisterhood environment. My struggle, living on my own mind, without anyone to debate progressive ideas, might make me sound childish or even naive to a level to few sorry for. Facts of life. I am not worried about being judged but the prosecution for uncommitted crimes change my sleep sometimes.

5) Some of the texts were written as if it was to another person who might lives in the silence of thoughts. A kind of an ode for a friend, who is not in my real (touchable) life. Placed in a nice corner of my mental guilty pleasure space. A Jack in a box, where there is always someone there, who should't be there, at all.

It's a kind of women's porn, acting like a fetich. Dong dong from a guitar triggering the opening up of this forgotten Jack. It also can be seen as a little cherry, in the middle of the day-by-day blues, to make it sweet.

"The same way a man search for his illusions on any porn hub, girls got their desirable fuck material too!" Sentence recorded from "A martini too many" afternoon!

A thousand wrong ways to see a situations spinning together with a cyclone of unnecessary words, confessing so much more than what it was requested. "Illusiones", like the published book from 1977!

6) How our brains cope with the pressures of the post covid times a-heading for the changes in culture and society behaviour. Is there any room for romance in 2022, in our easy dating app generation? Are we the last kind of humans, fully free to express romantic love before tech-modifications take it away from us, in the upper coming future? If all this is true, only time will tell!

There is, also, a combination of tales, from other friends. They are all female, exploding hormonal waves, probably turning into crazy bitches, on every full moon! Ages from 24 to early 50s, girls are bleeding no matter the stage in life. Yeap! We are almost going mad out there! Here I am bagging on the door again, calling science to help us, in the journey to understand, how to tame the fires from the hell of hormonal changes. Am I a dreamer?

7) I recognised myself as my own soulmate (most of the time), said that, the fires are still in need to develop into refined kundalini activation modes. The mind is easy to be aligned once synchronised vibrations take place. So far the heart is the one missing to be real.

Music is the strongest way to my pumping enthusiasm.

The unhidden note to a hidden thrill where silence only counts as my loss! Nothing to forget or forgive.

I'll take the shame and walk away to the sun.

Celebrations with a cake, made with the dark dust from the broken heart valley, laughs to swallow the pride and from now, I wish only naughty treats, please?

The "Happy ever after" concept only started 150 years ago, so let's embrace fate against my wishes and move on.

Welcoming myself back home.

The Death of romantic love is happening pretty much, in love!

Whatever kind of love it might be, it's transmuting big time!

Free written to keep it calm but not necessarily cool!

Cheers!

(The numbers were only items to ignore, once they were here just to add confusion.)

———————————

■■ "Hush - Original Mix" La Dame Noir.

~~Cindy and her past.~~ are waiting
for a healthier vagal tone.
Harbinger of past despair.
Losing the sense of individuality
looping into recover to get wasted
again while moving forward.
She writes and heals on heels…
…her heels!

The vagal nerve is the longest and most complex of the 12 pairs of cranial nerves that emanate from the brain. It transmits information to or from the surface of the brain to tissues and organs elsewhere in the body.

13

Foreign Love.

The brave that wages foreign wars,
shall harvest the glories in the land of the rose.
The soul was never to return to Africa
but the words were spoken beyond illusions.
The first king of Life protects his prodigal daughter, with his sword.
7 years are teaching cavalry to lead the knights into battles.
Her dark look observes when Ogun baptises a blond, blue-eyed man.
The widespread attribution of the red cross, bleeding from her vain,
in an union.
One clap, silence and she whispers with an accent:
"The circle of trust once broken
Ends the fire coming from my dragon's purr."

"The Last Living Rose" PJ Harvey.

14

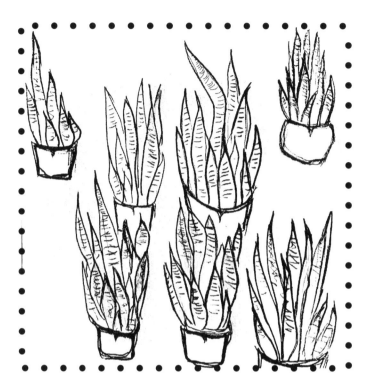

Dracaena Trifasciata.

Long time around me, extending your shield and your arms.
Feeding me with your strength and your greatness.
One day, I might see my enemies underneath your feet become
humble and submissive…
…To your Saint George's sword.

"Brotherhood of the Misunderstood" Red Axes.

"Let's Have A Ball Tonight" Tim Maia.

3 = 1

One is represented by images that are in the dark.
Another strong blink is a rehearse for the next chapter of many lives.
The last, which was the first, then the previous two. (Wowing myself!) It's mad and confusing, edging lack of grammatical correctness.
Just to simplify the equation, some of them are just forgotten faces living in boxes, already delivered to the far memories storage centre.

To finish the longest chapter of life. I'm so far proving once again that forever can be achieved if merged into friendship.
It is always from one best friend to another!
Many hearts, bodies and souls which today fill up my modest book, what once was a catalog of broken promises.

Shipping slash skipping the unnecessary dramas, evolving free to be what I want to be, and letting them to manifest their own desires. Single married to hormonal turmoils. Time.

How long is it left to fall in love again?
I wish to all my ex-partners in crimes the best sex and romantic life ever!

As a record keeper and a storyteller I could also act like a museum to collect and maintain past dramas. It's not the case for the way I perceive and act in romantic relationships. I just let them go!

■ "Moment" Frankie Knight.

Using different types of medias I contemplate life siting on my pride. The idea of freedom comes from trust, which empowers self-expression. It is very interesting in words, but real life strikes hard again and again. Let's not build up more oppression! Time vindicates everybody! We are all just kids!

Present? I am.
When the minor key reverbs, the songs vibrate my wishes towards you. Shakespearian scribbles helped to shape dreams, so far away from all those beloved freaks from the past.

It's our panel for freedom, from versus chorus versus, guessing what will be written on our stones.
Fast, hungry completing the art work for a new life.
My 3 to become 1. Why are we never 2?
Then, so far, it is just 0 for all of us!
Once again, the last was the first but between the previous 2.
Breathing in and out. One-night stand smiles don't make a rainbow!

Just because I can do whatever I desire It doesn't mean, I should! Inside the scope of sense, I say to you:
Bring the grunge, suck my blood and fly butterfly!

■ "Two Against One" Danger Mouse & Jack White.

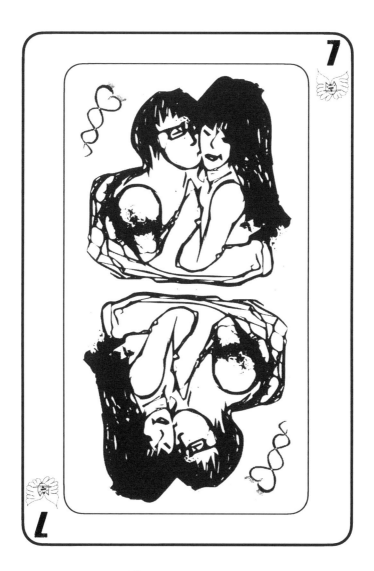

■ "I Don't Know" Beastie Boys.

Hair under concrete and white
A step backwards for you
 A triumph for me and the time goes by.
Winky Thursdays into your fear of the ''what if'… '
…what if… she bangs your drums?'

"I am a Madman" Lee Scratch Perry

20

I love Thursdays

Trembling lips
Clap your hands once again
Vibrating that Resonant silence of the guilt
Aware plunging hopes in pastel blue and black

Guitar riffs and the way we sync
Charging all energy for the twisted
Happiness revisited
Every atom dances in a flash
Turning tables to turn tumbles
Collider of happiness coming back home

I love Thursdays
Until the second cocktail I bet
We are all masks and gloves!
Cheering to the perfect ambassador
buying happiness on our alcoholic day.
Tonight I'm getting what is mine

Thursday's bests!
Thursday's breathes
Thursday's Bets
It's hard to beat.
Thursday on Thursday
Hard is the beat on Thursdays

Sometimes at night
all comes to place
The pressures are off
I love Thursdays

———————————

"Screen" Brad

22

The combination of secrets hidden in riddles.

Very savvy and intelligent women are victims of their own mind and
body misunderstandings. Hormonal hell!
A lot of crazy body changes, that we have no control over, places
many of us, wrongly, as over thinkers. Here we choose the most
important subject when it comes to life. Money? No! It's about Love.

Romantic love was considered a mental illness issue, that many
intellectuals and academics from the past, would fear like the plague.
Platonic love is a subject that I have read about for many years, so my
friendship with Cindy has always grown stronger, since I met her in
Brazil in the early 90s. We are cold as ice to self-analyze!

We can rewrite this paradox, where people end up becoming or doing
toxic things based on a pre-programmed mind by observing their
parents' failure.

My true painted life, similar to a chess board,
could be very easy if I'd followed the rules shaped by society.
However, mastering how to place myself as queen and king in
perfect synchronism not be knocked down, is hard.
It requires a lot of resilience, investment and dedication.
If one component of the board misbehaves, the full picture is fucked.
If there is no partnership and trust, between the queen, bishop and the
tower everything you builded up can break flat and you get lost.

I drank all the poison like shots of pro secco and now, I am so
peaceful if compared to a year ago! I learned that many times is wiser
just to SHUT THE FUCKING HELL UP POLLY!!

Everything happens at the right time anyway!
We think we have control of things. Ha! Such a silly sausage!

I'd like to apologise, especially to myself in the future:
*"Dear me, if I am still slow pace to get some peace of mind,
It's not because I am a coward....
...I am a mother! "*

■ "Lotus" R.E.M.

"Fly On the Windscreen" Depeche Mode.

24

Everything that involves the idealisation of another body and soul.

Modern Life with old fashion drives.
Diminished in strength, one part of the party is always searching for what is missing.
Are you the one? The One? What ta fuck is the fucking one?
How many "Ones" are in need of giving up seeking, for this imaginary ideal of one day, to becoming whole again?
Where is Home from here?

Your sounds give the tools to guide the blind force so attracted to the unknown. Idealisation is immersed with the lack of repeated exposure.
Oh, was Zeus playing a game when ordered to separate body and soul? Are humans all spaced, rolling two sides forgetting that one day we were one?
Mythology and experienced personal soap operas helped to maintain the utopia of finding someone who could see me.
My mirrors are just for one! The one is me!

Old chivalry tales give space for present expectations versus signs of time. 2022 is not the same as in 1998 in terms of reasons we couple up with possible romantic partners.

We live in the era of Tinders; we can easier swipe out of a catalog who we can have for the night. To be a woman and have fun, seems it was never so easy! Ah, such a shame, that Cindy, my other friends and I don't like it easy!

■ "Contact" Jarvis Cocker.

25

The key is to play your cards right with yourself.

"The One" was inside you all along! It's not about those blue eyes you wish for… It is your own light being recognised by yourself. I feel I am worth it so much more than I get. I am not really up to engaging in shaking my peacock feathers, if the rewards seems too much effort, for no fun at all. Contradictory to the last sentences, I wrote books about these utopias and illusions.

My guilty pleasure always was to fix my attention on only one person at the time. Sex has little to do with romantic love, but it does develop the state of belonging and dependency, if the action is worth the agro!

Cultural modern values overwrites romantic love. It challenges the thoughts, where is it really necessary to fall in love in order to feel happy?

It should never be the main focus, this searching for something imaginary; instead of learning how to overcome our own personal unfinished business, let's try to make it useful.

Isn't it naive to project personal frustrations on someone else, expecting to be given the fulfilment of what is missing in your own personal growth?

Knowing about the logistics of enlightenment does not make the journey easier.

I don't need a man to say to me how amazing I am, said that; please, tell me why do I put effort into attracting the attention of someone who clearly, needs more attention than me?

I tried to avoid the piercing blue eyes that I felt for so many times. Again, my internal battle with the fire I breathe.

The princess is no longer waiting for whoever is winning the match, because she clocks who owns the whole kingdom!

"3,000 Miles" Champs.

26

Right, Cindy says *"Ahh what a pain!! I fucking dislike princesses! It's so boring, tacky!"*
"Fair play!" I reply! *"We don't get on with princesses because we are two fucking DRAMA QUEENS!!"*

Nobody tells us about kissing a lot of frogs before finding a prince. Even worse, normally we kiss a Prince who turns into a frog with time. That's a well-known outcome of modern romance for sure but then, a mix of a frog and a prince can turn into something even more dense and different. Yeap, shit definitely happens, darlings!

Welcome to The Death of Romantic Love.
When the river dries down between your Canyons.
When the touch becomes an insult.
Agro? (agro and toxic?)
Pardon the pun, if there was one!
Many jokes to wash the bitterness away.
Now we are here waiting for the final wave!
Surfing away amicably!
(Oh, what an irritating word!)
It's an exchange between our deep values and beliefs shifting to the cold cruelty of rejection. If you believe in "Live and let live", no harm has been done.

Ah, confrontation is not on the agenda to some troubled people, who are hard to see sense to a level that I considered starting to believe in paranormal activities! Only such a thing can explain how they can keep themselves alive! Easier to make yourself blind to all this confusion in the air. Eyes wild open on the phone, but brain close down because somebody is the one, out of order here!

"Still Life" The Horrors.

27

Many of my friends are getting divorced and those singles ones are all engaged to an imaginary person, normally someone online, who they never even met!

No valentines for so many couples struggling with personal freedom. In a mix of some of the conversations I remember, here I got some of the pearls for comedy:

"Oh, I see. Was he talking to a magpie? He gambles! The bastard is a gambler!"
"He became she, but he doesn't like wigs!"
"The desirable ghost doesn't sing anymore!",
"Ill punch him in the face, if Amsterdam was nice!
"My mother wants a dildo for her 79 years old pussy"

All the sentences above can be translated to:
"No one is fucking!" At least not for free or because it is wanted or desired. Some people prefer to pay for a blow, putting the powder in someone else's nose, on an empty trip to nowhere! Fair enough, if you can not use your head, pay for a hand!

We are just part of a bigger madness. I have enough of the blues, the moaning, the headaches, it is so boring! What did we get out of the fake Pandora's box?

Why is no one laughing if the clock is still ticking?
Are we friends by joy or by trauma?
Many minds and hearts are involved.
I can only say it's not a bad thing; it's just life!
Would you like to jump on a trip with me?
Everything starts ONLY after a clear invitation from you.
If I say yes, be sure, it's a karma coma connection!!

"Feet" Fat White Family

Oh, I really think about you when the little I know the better
it is. A vicious circle was sabotaging myself when I asked
too much. "Hormonal urgencies" to fuck like porn stars.
Deep inside I want you to get this right.
Don't forget the gin, slap me, kiss me like it is the last kiss
of your life, make me laugh and be devoted to the sound of
my voice, all at the right time! Here is my recipe to our
disaster, contradicting the truth of being just angels
disguised as dark and lust!

I can write a thousand words while singing a song to you.
At the end of the day you are not listening but you might
read! Gently licking your lips I tell you, don't stop!

I got plenty of gibberish to entertain you and your troops for
long winters. Following the rhythm from the song we wrote
about tantric encounters, it goes easy like:
"Come close to me... to turn it on!"

"Facts of Life" Talking Heads.

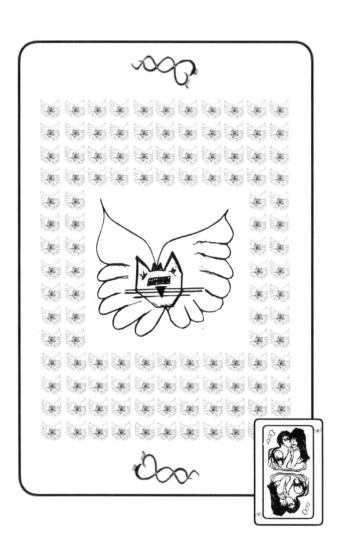

"First Kiss" Tom Waits.

<u>It's my sin to find intelligence sexually attractive and arousing.</u>

Confessing it really takes my views away from those wet patches
on a dirt t-shirt coming out from a building site.
All the superficiality, where our looks are prized above all else.
Challenge thoughts are so old fashion these days.
I felt like I was in a cult!
To have sense of time.
A world without spontaneity,
I hope, it will never to be possible.
Now 02-02-2022 @ 02:20
Tea and bed!

■∙• "My Body is a Cage" Arcade Fire.

"Please, Please, Please, Let Me Get…" The Smiths.

■ "I Wanna Be Adored" The Raveonettes.

Playful like a ghost DJ on Spotify poem.

"Cosmic Dancer" T.Rex.

(YOU ARE)
COMING CLOSE TO ME WITH
THE RUSH OF A SEA HORSE!
TWO AGAINST ONE GRIM RECEIVER
NEVER SAW IT COMING
FELT IN MY GUTS!
MY BODY IS A CAGE,
WHERE STIL LIFE LIVES.
NO WAR & BREATHE DEEP
PANCAKES FOR ONE →
ALL TOO SOON BUT MILES AWAY
DANCERS IN DAY DREAMING
HEY YOU! LONG GONE WITH WILD FLOWERS
IN THIS TWILIGHT RESERVATION
INSIDE OUT I CALL YOUR NAME
LIKE A BAD GIRL SHOULD!/
FIRST KISS.. I DON'T KNOW!

"A La Plage" Juniore.

Cigarette kisses

Cigarette Kisses bring the idea of enjoying small guilty pleasures and others pearls without a reason to be taken too seriously. I like to talk about the stars, souls, mind, sun and the sea for well-being. I do rituals in my house to harmonise the auras of the cats using music. I'm also very miserable in the morning depending on what happened in the night before. To be honest, people like me have to use everything to calm down the nerves in a world full of fucking idiots! Said that I am also an idiot myself (sometimes), so don't get offended.

I enjoyed my time at educational institutions like school, college/universities, night clubs and music festivals.
Even today, I go to the health club to spend an afternoon in a sauna, just talking bullshit with the people talking bullshit. Quality dramas and gossips on my local sauna! It justifies paying the membership just to get free access to common people's views of mundane life.

I learned about different religions, even if I am not a religious person myself. My friends were like an 80's advert for Benetton. My parents home was always full of many kinds of opinions. My father was a fantastic thinker compared to my mother, who is still pretty much like a wild animal.

I miss the conversations with my dad, when we would almost daily, starting from the newspaper in the morning, then late evening politics debates and financial analyses or listening to the talk radio. Many times my friends would participate in having some tea.

"Sea Horse" Devendra Banhart.

The Death of Romantic love is my way of talking to myself once I no longer have late-night talks with my father. Sometimes England can be colder than death, exactly like love. My own gain or loss.

My husband says that life is shit then you die. I just got in the back of my mind, (LIFE IS SHIT then YOU DIE x4), boom boom, is it a punk soundtrack for a divorce?
Enough about No politics, No sex, No society, No going to the beach, No dinner parties, No sleeping together in the same room, No deep conversations, No Yoga, No massages, No spiritualism (HAHAHA maniacally laughing now!!),
NO let me cook in silence while listening to the radio, and
It goes on, compromising trips in our compromised still life.

Important detail (for myself in the future), my husband is a passive-aggressive type. Quiet, he is a musician for fun, but his knowledge of making music and his hearing are exquisite. It doesn't mean he listens to me! Said that, which man does listen to us anyway?
We are still making music together and that seems to be a point that works alright. We are good band mates in silence. I want to believe we are friends! Badly I want to believe I am doing the right thing.
My internal argument grows when I work to stop bad habits. The blackness of my heart, does not justify staying stuck in the same shit repeatedly. If I have a problem with him, the problem is mine! Nothing new, but the responsibility of success, only comes apparent to the eyes after a long cold trail of tries and failures in the loneliness of the dark. Something to figure out myself for sure! Swim or sink?

A fraction of discipline in a daily routine should include some "Cigarette kisses conversation", to help to shift the view of being a victim of life, in a try to recognise the steps of manifesting a better way to feel good within yourself.

Breaking my concentration, then I remember the point where I was writing about how the planets and the sun helps me to cope if the FUCKING MORGUE THAT IS MY LIVING ROOM AFTER DINNER!!AAAAAAAAHHHHHHHHHHHHHHH
Somebody stop this train cos I want to jump out!
It's so easy to have a strong emotional effect on my behaviour, not being competitive enough to work when the void takes place. Questions embracing the overwhelming confusion come in bulks almost like daily.
What happened to me? I thought that I was a bubbly! Fucking hell, what a boring cunt I became! What have I done? What or WHO do I think I am? Who Am I?
Have a word!! Oh, please give me words!

After the burst of frustration because of the lack of normal conversation previous to dinner. I just want to leave recorded in here facts as they happened. I am writing this soon after the stress. I want to let myself know that I just need to ignore the machine. Everything will be ok tomorrow; this discomfort will pass.

I see myself burning my dignity like an inquisition in my own mind. The devils are several cans of beer, porn addiction, and cold emptiness. Right, counting resiliences 1, 2, 3, 4. I think I need some tea, a spliff, let me think about an illusion (not a sexual one otherwise I'll get more frustrated now), and read about crypto currency. Did you buy Shibba Uni?
I welcome the children of the past echo. See you in 2027!

Ah, I got mirrors everywhere. I have been obsessing about mirrors since I was born. I love my image. My mother hated the way I love everything about me. I acknowledge that I sound like a right arse now. Ah, I wish to be a comedian! At least if I was funny to hit the core of a subject in a single laugh! Ta! Just another dream or my lack of deeper studies about the mind.
My discomfort allows me to see my progress.

39

"C.R.E.A.M." El Michels Affair.

It is not what it seems! Come on, Cindy. You got to get the focus back. *"Ah, those arms cracking the chicken for the barbecue! STOP!!"* Her mind drift away daydreaming once again. Come on, get back here! T.E.A. where is my TEEEEA take the fucking camomile infused with "Lexotan" and gin!!

Cigarette Kisses are comfortable.
There is an element almost like that pillow talk, a trust feeling involved. It's the mind bond, connections of ideas, music or name it what you like. It is the excitement of having a moment with someone who is an enjoyable companion.

Cigarette Kisses can be gossiping without deep bitchiness, talking about left-wing's power or watching cartoons drunk after a night out.

I do study a lot about mind and body balance. Countless time I have been writing about music vibrations and the impact of positive thinking got over the tiny daily disappointments. Practice it all with my cats and walls.
The dialogue, that I can not have with anyone around comes out into a calm and sweet tone of my voice while combing my hair. Love the skincare routine! Normally mornings are to listening to my pals and the news of the dirt world, feed by Instagrams and Facebook's bullshit. People are all overloaded with their problems. When I see my friends I want to have a good time with them, and not necessarily, tell them about my stresses. The future is to be quiet!

Clap my hand as a command to change the subject.
Cigarettes and Kisses fusing daydreaming plus facts from a real past life?

It goes like this:

41

"She was already biting lips, quick as the light. Clocking the primitive move of his right hand over his paints. Painfully holding the face muscles in a try to look cool when tingling with happiness.

She is as cool and dark as his dirtiest wishes on a perfect mad sex explosion. He is dry and fast to break the ice releasing that beautiful face into laughs to cackling. The long reunification cuddles from now forever in their minds (regardless if forever will only be there until it lasts). Breathing each other's hair aware the presence of their frequency fixing the milestone from and for both paths.

Even if those eyes were closed closer like when listening to the guitar dong".

Dong dong.

This is it. I'm gonna finish it well, later.

It was just random thoughts written in a trance to fight against this boredom.

Cigarette Kisses are what I miss the most.

To finish the subject I'll write some lyrics for a song.

■ "Cigarette Kisses" These Cats Don't Give A Fuck!".

42

CIGARETTE KISSES
RUN TO LIFE, HOUSEWIFE!
HOW TO TRUST?
THE LIPS TOUCHED

CIGARETTE KISSES
ADDICTIVE TASTE OF FUN
ESCAPING FROM MONO, INVADING MY STEREO
TO SHAKE UP A SCENARIO
ON CHERRY AND CHERRIO, ONE PISTACCHIO!

CIGARETTE KISSES
SUCK MY BLOOD
SWALLOW ME ONCE AGAIN
SEND ME A SONG TO BE AWARE
WHEN CONTAIN CHAMPAGNE,
BUT BETTER NOT TALK COCAINE,
COS I'M ALWAYS ON A PLANE.

CIGARETTE KISSES
INSANE MEMBRANE
WHEN WHISPERING SHE SAYS
CIGARETTE KISSES
CAGE AWAY MY GRUDGES
CIGARETTE KISSES
BRUISES THIS MISTRESS
CIGARETTE KISSES
PUT ME OUT OF THE BUSINESS
CIGARETTE KISSES
RUN TO LIFE,
YOU, ORDINARY HOUSEWIFE!

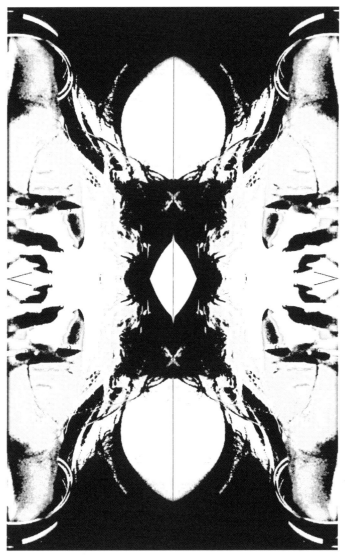

■ "Au début c'était le début" The Limiñanas & Laurent Garnier.

That was an example of how to
cope in moments of crisis!

Sometimes when MENstruation
tint my days, the following
observed pattern might occur:

Money worries
Zen-Chi Force
Meditation
Cleansing
Camomile tea
CBD or weed
Music
Hash
Horny in the mirror
GIN
Bread sticks
Frustration
Tantrums
Tears
Phone
Comfort
Comparison
Laughs
Online Shopping
Dark Chocolate
Ibuprofen
I love my life
Sleep
Snore
Wake Up
Start all over again!

"Gotta Get A Grip - Kevin Parker Remix" Mick Jagger.

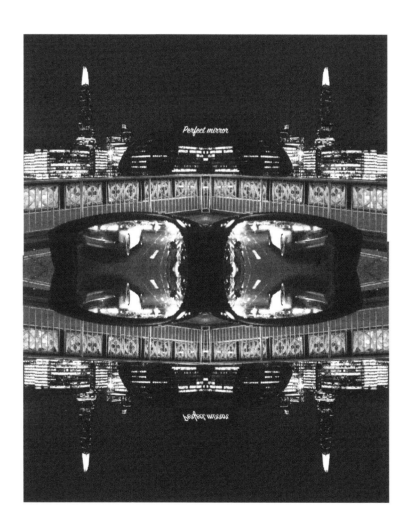

47

Standing Still

Who lives in your mind
When you come undone?
All alone ain't much fun,
Then we are looking for a thrill.
Using my try to make patterns
Rhyme, like a new romantic.
Is this the last exit before
the turn to individualism?
I'm always dancing into the fire!
The phoenix for the flame,
Collecting minds to hearts
overseas... standing still!

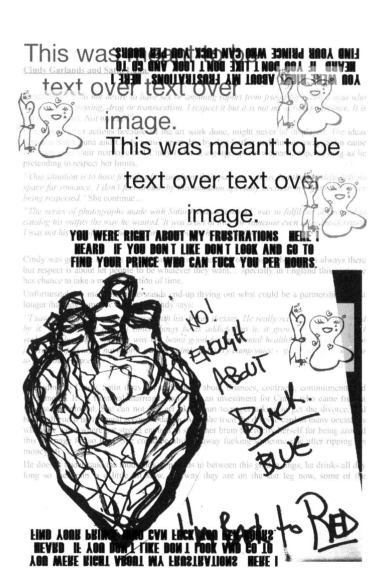

This was ... text over text over image. This was meant to be text over text over image.

YOU WERE RIGHT ABOUT MY FRUSTRATIONS HERE I HEARD IF YOU DON'T LIKE DON'T LOOK AND GO TO FIND YOUR PRINCE WHO CAN FUCK YOU PER HOURS.

NO! ENOUGH ABOUT BUCK BLUE

Back to RED

"You Want It Darker" Leonard Cohen.

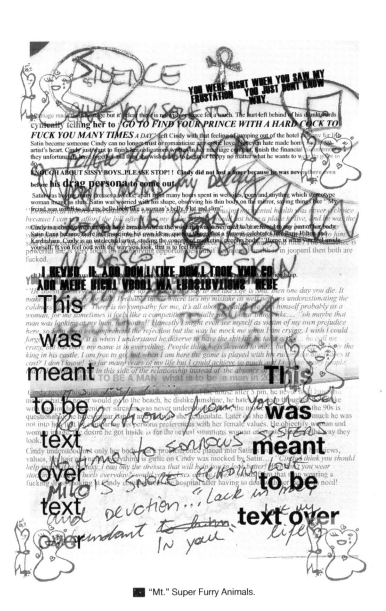

Marriage made us in bondage but it's clear there is no wish or space for a touch. The hurt left behind of his drunk words cynically telling her to *'GO TO FIND YOUR PRINCE WITH A HARD COCK TO FUCK YOU MANY TIMES A DAY'"* left Cindy with that feeling of jumping out of the hotel balcony for life. Satin become someone Cindy can no longer trust or romanticise any erotic love. Hate even hate made home, hate has an artist's heart. Cindy just want to finish her obligations written in her marriage contract, finish the financial commitment they unfortunately have together and then she wishes him to be super happy no matter what he wants to wear in order to do.

ENOUGH ABOUT SISSY BOYS...PLEASE STOP!! Cindy did not lost a lover because he was never there even before his drag persona to come out.

Satin was buying many dresses a weeks, apart from many hours spent in websites, porn and anything which stereotype woman image as sluts. Satin was worried with his shape, observing his thin body on the mirror, saying things like "My freind was usulal to say my belly look like a woman's belly, flat and slim"... using his mental health was never a choice because I can you afford the bill after all... my... would eat have a place to live, and he was the m... Cindy is a chubby woman with huge breasts where the word that was never med to be referred to any part of my body, Satin cuna become more and more into his own ideas, quoting things that a famous celebrates like Paris Hilton do to him Kardashian. Cindy is an intellectual artist, studing the concept of marketing peoples body. "Home is what you feel inside yourself, if you feel ood with the way you look, that is to feel home... powerful she is... focus on... living opportunity... loved... him in jeopard then both are fucked.

I NEVER IT ADD DOM I LIKE DOM I TOOK WHO CO
ADD MERE RICHL VROOL YM LUBCIBVANNS HERE

"He doesn't seem to understand that you only stay to me the like is Shit, then one day you die. It makes... for fair. Probably this is where lies my mistake as well perhaps underestimating the coldness... There is no sympathy for me, it's all about equality, to see himself probably as a woman, for me sometimes it feels like a competition specially when I wear things like... "oh maybe that man was looking at my bum, not yours!! Honestly I might even see myself as victim of my own prejudice here, so far, so... to comprehend the rejection but the way he mock me when I am crying, I wish I could forge... it is when I understand he deserve to have the shit life he talks ... he call me crazy, but each time my name is in everything. People think he is devoted to me, but... he feels like king in his castle, I am free to go, but when I am here the game is played with his rule... at what... cost? I don't know! So far many years of my life but I could achieve so much and I also so... people... in this side of the relationship instead of the absence...

This was meant to be text over text

TO BE A MAN, what is to be a man in 2...

Cindy... the... that... house after 5 pm, he never... hang... m... that... never would go to the beach, he dislike sunshine, he hate... so... though... take with... the... ever sarcasm was never under... the... 90s is questionable, he hates guitar band and... she... articulate, Later on she... much he was not into he... but like comparing his persona preferences with her female values. He objectify woman and woman image, the desire he got inside is for the sexual situations woman on... the way they look...

Cindy understood not only her body was problem once placed into Satin... interviews, values, her hair and nails, everything is girtic on Cindy was mocked by Satin...! "Cindy... think you should help you... sexy, I can buy the dresses that will help you to look better! Won't you wear stach... heels everyday? I would you... sex... the... W D... him that I am wearing a fucking dress looking at Cindy coming from the hospital after having to deal... emer... need!

This was meant to be text over

"Mt." Super Furry Animals.

"Don't You Know " Jan Hammer Group.

"Dirge" Death In Vegas.

Days when the silence is invaded.

Iciness invaded Cindy's heart decades ago, so her days are fighting the right to party, which remains stronger than death!
Paranoias feeding on her discreet advantage points once lost in their game of guessing in the dark. What comes next?
The number of players on the board is far overdue. The firm.
Unlike most vampires, they descend on the route of friendship. She keeps them close to avoid the danger. It is quite a spectacle. Some of them sometimes flex their jaws, pretending to be bothered, in an alpha way of intimidation. Anyone wants more attention but once she smiles, they are all under the blast of her spell again.

Once the surroundings were safe, her fingers clenching around the material and vinyl, a song took her mind back to someone long gone. His voice is not whispering through her mind anymore.
Her exploits into the groove have a huge connection to him and have been intense since before they said hello. She was ashamed to admit that she wanted just a night with him. She felt very sexually attracted to him since day 1. Unfortunately, her imaginary "Batman" was not interested in her as much as she appreciated. She was not fully there either, so no regrets as long as he is quiet in his corners.
Any encounters between them have far more chances, to guarantee a few laughs and jokes for a day, rather than any drip of combined sweets as consequences of passion and lust.

Cindy is more scared of perpetuating her misery rather than taking risks to rewrite her story.
We all bolt in panic when actions are required upon our fates.
To understand her place within any romantic relationship, we invested some time in the question: Is she a harmony seeker disguised as a heart breaker? Or is she pretending to be a nice person to end up fucking someone else's brain? There is a thin line between casual relationships that can make people insane.

What to do when you are feeling unattractive because a duck did not say hello to you?

 "Ashes To Ashes " Warpaint.

Let's start with a tiny change a day. It's ok to focus on her illusion with him, but it was just meant to be a little bit of imaginary fun. Cindy asked "Why doesn't he write to me? Following her question, she carried on, speaking her mind and giving me a list of possible reasons for him, not asking her out.
Here they are followed by my observation in italic:

1. He got someone else! (*He does not want to have a simple chat with you! It doesn't matter who he is with! That's not a priority for you!*).
2. He is busy! (*Nope, there is no fucking busy man there. He never said that to her, because he never says anything ever!*).
3. He is a clever man, sniffing the scent of a drama queen on the horizon. (*I think he has a good sense of self-preservation!*).
4. He is not interested. (*This is like "a biblical first command" that neutralises any other commands. It's a blessing that he is not interested! Imagine if he knocked on your door? I bet you'd avoid him, because soon he comes close, you are no longer interested! It's just desirable because he is not on his knees doing everything you say so*).

Countless times I try to bring her to my senses, reminding her that illusions are just to make ourselves become better for ourselves! Her dream fuck, might be a nice gentleman, but he is not an option to repair her heart, mind or any past traumatic experiences with her previous romantic partners. Just last winter she was a heck. I imagine the WhatsApp apocalyptical messages that she sent to him after a few drinks! The guy is sensible, not contacting her at all.

Sometimes it's better to be complacent and not follow dreams, which are consequences of badly interpreted illusions. This platonic love is doomed since the conceptualisation of them as a couple! The right thing is to stick to what she knows, to avoid a tone of trouble starting! Now she can wish him well, accepting he is not for her!

The drop of the coin made her see, she was already happy with his silence, but she didn't even know it. She wonders about him, but it's not a life-changing situation. He is just a daydreaming cherry!

Recording day

Studio
28/10
2021

Faithful
In
love
with
myself
Again ♡

TURN
ME
ON
BABY!

Our

Sounds AND

Waves

YOUR HAIR
MY HAIR
WHEN YOU ARE WATCHING the SEA

I'm STONGER
I'm STONGER
THINKING OF YOU.

CLICK
HERE
THE
METRONOME !!

Come CLOSE TO ME... 4X
Come CLOSE...

VERY
quiet!

Come BACK TO US. ME
COME BACK... TO TURN IT ON!!!

"3D Warrior" Nightmares On Wax.

59

NÃO CAGUE NO PAU, REGINA!

My friends and I use this sentence when it comes to the territory "I'm interested in having sex with a person I don't know that well, but I'm feeling it."
In the very rude, grotesque and direct translation... "Don't skid on his cock, Regina!" It works as an allusion to knowing that you are going to have anal sex and in the excitement, you don't clean your ass well before the action! The expression is connotative, only to directly express the feeling of saying some nonsense that can drive the interested person away, rather than attracting them to your bed. It is when you over portray yourself as a needed cow.

Every woman talks some nonsense when she's dealing with a guy whom she has a strong crush. In addition, it also includes projecting oneself poorly or exaggerating silence. Every woman has her own way of "Shitting on the dick" Cagar no pau, Regina!.

Rule number 1 of the club, "Don't skid on his dick, Regina?" Just stay away from the most dangerous, terrible and feared of modern life, our ultimate real enemy: Mr. Whatsapp, mother fucker!! Mobile phones + alcohol are not friends with the person who doesn't want to "Shit on his dick". If you drink, NEVER write anything.

My friend and her colleague got really drunk in a hotel while they were on a business trip. Once she was alone, the idiot started sending voice messages to the person she got something going on (on her mind). He doesn't even know she is into him. He doesn't even remember her existence!

"Careless Whisper" Eagles Of Death Metal.

She sent a huge voice message and deleted it soon after. Then she sends another one... another one. There were sixteen voice messages!! Sixteen messages! All erased and in the end, just a stupid, stupid phrase like "I just wanted to send you a song."

She was lying naked in a wonderful bed; she was very drunk and watching porn thinking about the guy she had just voicemails on WhatsApp. Anyway, she had a fantastic orgasm looking in the mirror. After that, she ate a small piece of chocolate and fell asleep.

In the morning after, when she got up, the coin dropped... *"What the fuck did I do last night on this WhatsApp?!!* 16 deleted messages... *"What a psycho!!"*

In cases like this, the best advice is to call a friend.

It doesn't matter where a woman may be in the world. She can be underwater, in the air, driving, having sex, sleeping, working or even inside a hospital but when a friend sends the general alert code, the emotional distress call, we are always ready to laugh at the shit.

What is the code that all the girls send to each other?
"Help...CAGUEI NO PAU, REGINA."
Always will be a sister there just to talk about your shame!

"I Found Love" Shit Robot.

61

■ "Never Saw It Coming" Champs.

63

Resolutions 2000s

Under the moonlight
Our beautiful time
Exchanging jokes
Black and white
Like in a movie
Poetry about kraut
Swimming on high heels
Those bottles were collected
After a long tic-tacs in laughs!
The funny points of disagreements turned into
the foundations for an unforgettable New Year's Eve.
Some of those marvellous souls are not longer with us.
Extremely colourful balloons covering the pool.
We were hidden under water
Breathing with no eye contact.

The trip lasted longer than the disco.
Found around the trees our hair full of flowers.
The trinity of my mind and the sounds of the sunset
Dozen together for days of celebrations
even if they have never met before!
Candies and shots
Somebody was giving me Strawberries and Sake
Professional lenses pointed to my face,
Our profiles are the snapshots of fun.
Long plan for what suppose to be just another pop-up holiday
We were all DJing in the jungle!
Everybody was somebody but together we were kids!
Happy New Year forever!

My love to those lovers and all the brothers to this sister.

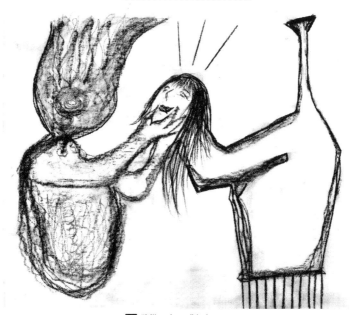

■ "Miles Away" Leisure.

"Hendrix Necro" Sonic Youth.

"Creme Brulee" Sonic Youth.

https://vimeo.com/639545804

Mojito Moms
Mojito bombs
Fight the boredom.
Mojito bomb
Mojito bombs

Losing my fate in solitude
Searching for the last berry
Drunken' doll bottoms up

Mojito bomb
Mojito bombs
Upgrade your thoughts
Sunset right next to the den
My famous street in silence
Nico and bananas were here

Mojito bomb
Mojito bombs

Mojito bomb
Mojito bombs
Yellow lights in my night
Peep bite for fish on tides

Mojito bomb
Mojito bombs
Thinking about the other half
Saving for the morning after
Here is always only me

Mojito bomb
Mojito bombs
Spin head come to bed
cuddle for the pillow talking
Gorgeous me.

Mojito boms
Mojito MOMS!

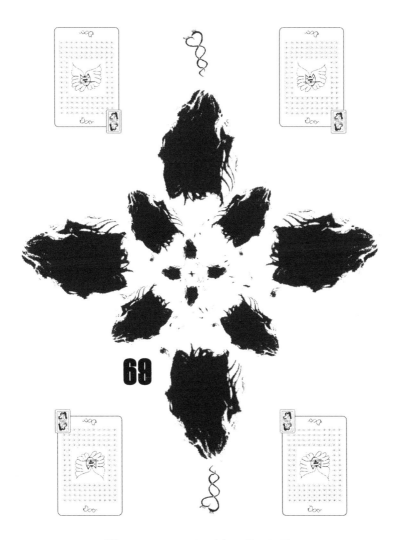

"Where The River Goes" Stone Temple Pilots.

Punishment and Protection

Erotic dreams flashed her day and she wished to call him now! All these portraits of her hidden self are not really giving the clues it supposes to.

Her art disguised in kraft (craft with K just because I can hide a few truths there), pure affliction materialised in cards, games, food, books and plane tickets. Back to me, I'm still writing about an idea, embarrassed to confess that I don't want any other. The tick-tack is getting fast upon the fact I know I can stop time.

Twilight rituals in nature I have been practicing everything. Shaping my future, to offer my power in the form of enlightenment (to myself, hahaha), with a cocktail of emotions. Clearly, I still know nothing, but it's more than I had yesterday! Sentences were written to be the fast spreader when Cobain couldn't vindicate me any way.

Then she heard when you disguised a note saying that things will never be the same again. I agreed completely, especially because they were never anything in the first place! A few days after, you were opening the line, slowing beats and bits to initiate the almost desirable communication from your shell.

Singing about the prettiest girl you've ever seen while the other workers downgrade yours exploits, melting in gossips, about all those Friday night hookers of yours.

Ah… boring! I couldn't care less!
Flashes of those cars in NYC at night, crossing my memories' avenues when you said, "It's all inside out."

A deal surfaces in the shape of unspoken promises as long she's here wanting "To be your bitch"!
(I was going to say dog just to play with Iggy, but it is very sophisticated to know about Stooges anyway).

It's our duty to fascinate the world. Real-life was painted using the opposite collars described in this rainbow of words. Annoying me to regret, he is not open at all! What to say? Bring it in. Amen… And she prays!… and prays for a potato! Cold nights and the fog in the morning to start a brand new story.

My insecurities makes me openly talk about them and even act upon them. Intense, but very Gemini, soft and free, as the love comes as easy it goes away too!
If the 2.7% is right, so I am one of them!
World leader pretend, here we go again!
Fuck me hard, but be aware:
I can break easily like crystal, but ain't no gullible!
I am made out of that dark onyx glow deep inside your eyes, only activated once intellectually aroused.
My punishment and Protection to a blessing or a curse?
Now you can just stare at this killer look.
Yeah! A dirty bastard!

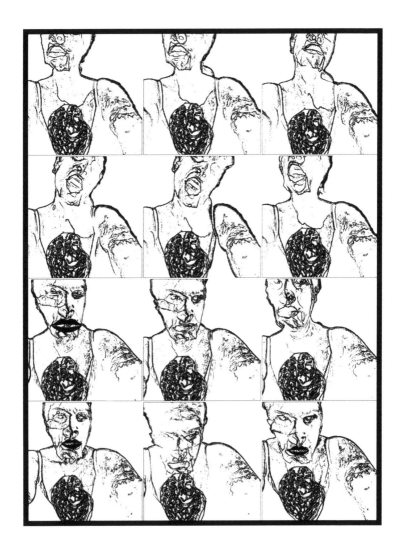

"I Want'a Do Something Freaky To You" Leon Haywood.

■ "Miss You" Mirwais.

73

"The Happening" Pixies.

Rolling on my fingers

The golden net little dress enables me to shape into shapes.
Dive quickly pointing directly to your thoughts with my up
tights limiting the round areas. Satin touch equals my furs.
Why do we hope to looking stunning regardless of the natural
confidence stamping the new image of these emotions?
You are always to get lost in here anyway.

Soft-biting applies the desirable pressure to this unicorn.
Bring out the wild from within. It's pulsing there.
What do you have to lose? Ah, what a questions!!
Unification of guilty pleasures perhaps two are made of
dreams and dramas, where out of the blues, everything seems
written about us.

I know you are breathing my stories like a spiced lullaby.
My voice over and over again like tinnitus tempting you to
break your promises, "Never do to someone what it was done
to you"! All my dreams and that tingling in the middle of your
legs and days are made of this. The moment before the given
in!

On your face or on my mind, both life and karma are knocking
on the door and soon after we open it up, it's all about
following the groove. Stroke the ego to strike my poses once
again.

Give me the words and the best angles of laughs, during and
after promises, avoiding that old burn taste of having to have
to kiss you goodbye.

■ "What Love" Jagwar Ma.

75

Bloom Serpent!

Hundreds of thoughts
Developing several lines of
Creative words from the absence of touch
Those peaceful hours while you were sleeping
Positive attitude reflects inner strength

Oh, self-help your arse!
Rude unexpected pleasing that little vanity of mine

Reality check has forgotten internal affairs of one soul
Into the congress of feelings, our portal for emotional bonds.
I work the invisible forces since birth.

Kiss me sweetheart, cause It's time to go to bed
Lucky morning strikes again, so our dreams have no sugar but
that wiggly pays the bills.

Dirty, kicking ways to increase the style
far beyond I imagine I could hit.
Bite your own tongue.
Bloom Serpent!

■ "Remember Me" Tame Impala.

3=1 (again) Thelema d' Amour.

Cold water on her face to dive into the
perceptions of present, oh…
''Vault of your arms and
arms to my body
to keep us alive.''

Moonlight helps her
to dish the message to the passenger,
Letting her know when he gets back to sense.

Written on the walls
dedicated to a Madman,
"Perhaps your mates might
know far less than she does."

Love of self and of others
The main base for mystical intoxication.

The way she moves her hair
Headphones and touches vinyl.
A distressed wimpy sound
Every time she thinks about him.
On a plane to Acapulco.

He is comfortable and dangerous; therefore,
she brings more than desirable troubles
but also a feeling of fullness that is so far gone.

3=1 Thelema d' Amour.
Zeus changed his mind and asked for some glue!

"Twilight Reservation" Tim Love Lee.

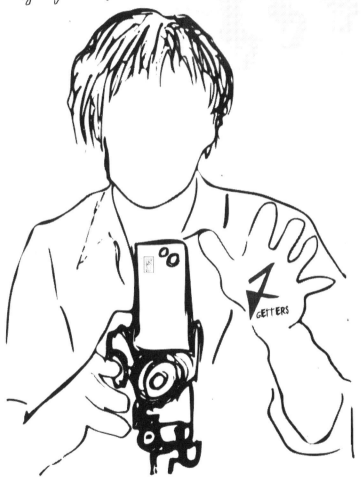

"The First Time" Scott Lavene.

**We ain't getting any younger; waiting for that
''right time'' that might never come.**

My conclusion:
It's better to be living while waiting to have a life.

"Vicious" Lou Reed.

DARK SEA
FREEDOM IS
MONEY AND CASH
FACE THE DEMON
IS NOT AN OPITON

DEEPER AND DEEPER
NOTHING WILL CHANGE
I WISH IT WAS ME...
SOMETIMES!

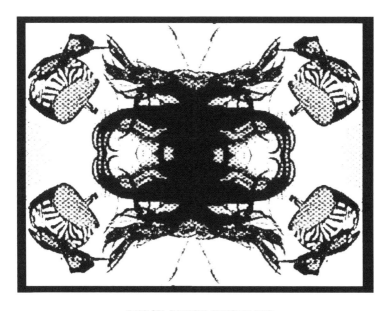

DARK SEA, DARK SEA, PLEASE BE KIND.
WHERE ONE DRESS IS FOR TWO
NOTHING WILL CHANGE THE PINK MARKS
WHEN THE WOOD IS DEAD

EVERYTHING BECOMES SO HEAVY
IT HURTS MY BACK SO MUCH
DIFFICULT TO SWIM WITH A GHOST.
THE WEIGHT OF A DEAD WOOD
DRAINS THE HOPE
OPENING UP THE TIME
FOR A CHANGE.

"Furious" Dawad, Mokic.

■■ "Venus" Roberto Rodriguez.

Pluto's Helmet

Brigitte is an academic French black woman who lives in Amsterdam.
She got two masters in economics and languages. She also owns a vegan restaurant.
Single, about 45 years old, she never would have kids.

Pamela (Pam) is a Swedish lesbian living in Spain. Doctor and a healer but everybody thinks she is just a boring charlatan.
She also works with luxury goods. She knows everything about blink and tacky sparkles. Everything has a name and surname, but not much depth.

Cindy is an American living in London. She is a lawyer and an musician. Business woman but seems nobody takes her seriously. She is a well-known arty personality.

Luna is an English person. Living in London is gender fluid. Sometimes they work as a model and other times as a plumber. Cash rich and very generous, they/he/she have/has a massive collection of cocktail dresses once he was married to Cindy.

All of them are wearing the "Pluto's Helmet" in order to speak truthfully.

Brigitte introduced the conversation: - *This restaurateur has been contacting me for 2 years... we are exchanging spiritual quotes and dark vegan secrets.*
Pam says as quick as a bullet: - *Spiritual quotes and dark vegan secrets!? Wow. Brigit, is the sex as deep as his gibberish?*
Cindy: *Oi, blonde! That's a bit harsh!*
Brigitte replies very naturally: - *Oh, he is not that kind of man. Dark secrets are food recipes... and also we haven't kissed yet!*

■ "Long Gone" Al Zanders.

Pamela and Cindy together: *-What? You never kissed him? Oh my Gosh!*
Brigitte said, *"He is a very complicated man. He is very busy working hard in the summer, to have some rest in the winter."*
Both were listening to all 20 minutes of the explanations to justify the 2 years delay in kissing considering the distance between Brigitte and her special friend's home is only 3 streets away.

Brigitti finishes with:
- I know he is in love with me but I don't know why it's taking so long for him to ask me out.
Cindy laughing, but not revealing much says:
- *Oh Boy! Oh, Boy! Is everybody in Europe having the same problems apart from Brexit? He might be just another member from the "Quiet in the dark club".*

Pam with a very slow and paused voice says:
- There is something wrong with this man. What is he waiting for?

Cindy gets finishing Pamela's sentence:
- Maybe he is not interested in real contact with you.

- It's hard to believe that a man in his 40s will delay to having free hot sex 3 streets away from his home for 2 years! Pamela said not giving time for Brigitti to reply.

Cindy waves to Luna (Cindy's ex-husband) to come to join them. Luna gets to learn all about Brigitte's dilemma. After listening to it all Luna looked straight at Brigitti and said:
- Does he like a bit of a sniff?

■ "Lonely Nights" Leisure.

84

- *Pardon?* Says Brigitti.
- *Does he like cocaine more than he fancies you?* Replies Cindy.
- *Oh... I don't know! Why is this connected to him not asking me out? I don't do drugs but I like vodka more than I fancy him! hahaha.* Brigi got the joke then Luna nailed it expressing her mind:
- *He probably got erection problems, maybe he is nervous about his cock!*

All the 3 of them looked at each other and the conclusion came.
''Wow, we never thought about it! Well, Luna has a cock. She knows what it is all about better than us!''
All agreed with Cindy nodding their heads and saying *''Yeap...I don't remember you blaming the drugs when your fella didn't work with me! Hahaha! Wow Brigit! Welcome to the valley of the forgotten powers.''*
Cindy said it all and they were already bursting to cackle...
Hahahaha
Pam finished:
- *He can buy a dildo in the shop close to the roundabout.*
- *...And that's the reason why I won't give up on him!*
Concludes Brigitti followed by a convoy of sounds from their unified cackling noises.

That was a silly dialogue between friends.
In Saint Marie, right next to a beautiful river
They were drinking French wine
and enjoying sardines.

Waters of 2021 from a spice summer.

———————————

"Chaise Longue" Wet Leg.

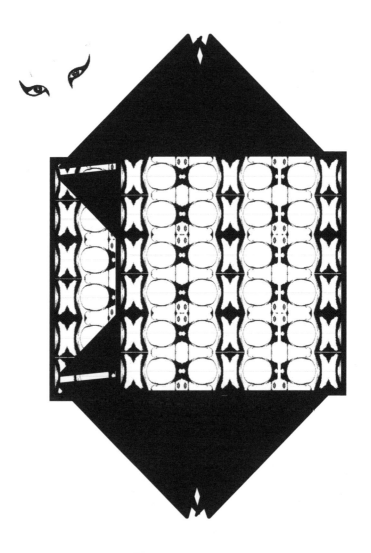

"Wild Flowers" Warmduscher.

86

ANOTHER HUNTER S MOON.
YOU LEFT ME HERE
WAITING FOR THAT
SILENT MOMENT
BEFORE THE GIVIN IN
WHEN
FACE TO FACE
SKIN TO SKIN.
COME ON,
STAND AND DELIVER.

COURO DE CU D ARSE.

"Sensations of Cool" Ttrruuces.

"Is it the best I can do?"
To put a pic of your arse in a book. Why not?
Cellulite is one of my oldest friends!
Yesterday's shame will be Tomorrow's glory!
Anamorphosis of my butt with kindness.

I know
everything about
your mind since
you told me by the
lyrics written from
indie hearts.

 "Grim Receiver" Shit Robot.

A Espera...

Esperando, comprou mais um vestido pra ele.
Esperando, vejo os olhos deles brilhando feliz enquanto ele se
olha no espelho.
Esperando, choro trancada no chão do banheiro.
Esperando, escuto que eu seria mais sexy se eu vestisse
vestidos bem curtos com salto alto.
Esperando, escuto que limites em momentos sexuais (na
opinião alheia) são como ser treinado como um cachorro.
Esperando, digo a ele que não quero mais fazer parte do anel.
Esperando, tiro fotos para deixá-lo mais feminino.
Esperando, escrevo contos de falso desejo carnal com coração
pleno de compaixão e simpatia
Esperando, respeito à liberdade dele de ser e de se sentir
amado como ele é.
Esperando, explico que o problema não é a obsessão dele com
vestidos e brinquedos
Esperando, lembro que não estou confortável e choro pedindo
pra ele apenas me deixar ficar calada.
Esperando, ele me diz pra ir procurar o meu príncipe
masculino que vai ter um pau duro pra me acalmar 3 vezes
por dia.
Esperando, escuto que meu jeito de me expressar é
inadequado
Esperando, escuto que essa minha cara triste com esse óculos
de velha não é nada bubbly

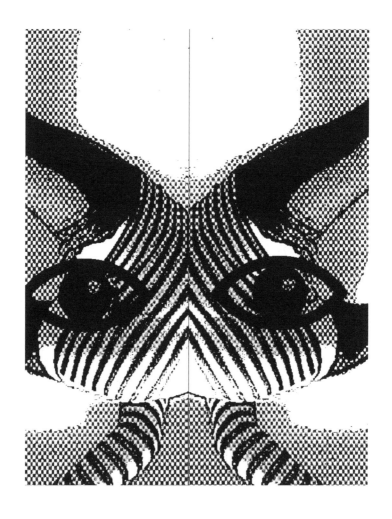

■ "Running Up That Hill" Chromatics.

Esperando, faço o café dele, um sanduíche e desejo que ele tenha um dia de boa sorte no trabalho.
Esperando, Fumo muito.
Esperando, aceito qualquer droga classe média que me deixe anestesiada e muda.
Esperando, toco os sons da caída do abismo esperando pra quando bater no fundo quicar pro seu barco
Esperando, escrevo sobre eu, você, ele, elas, nós e os gatos.
Esperando, converso com VOCÊ telepaticamente.
Esperando olhando pra ele me insultar eu agradeço pela música recebida que liberta minha alma.
Esperando você acontecer me preparo pra deixar o anel no cincerro e o sobrenome no conceito.
Esperando, sigo repetindo que não é você e nem ele
Esperando me sinto sempre sozinha.
Esperando, olho em outros olhos mas não consigo encher mais ninguém.
Esperando você cansar de me esperar, rezo pra vir bater na minha porta
Esperando, escrevi alguns livros, uns cheios de morte e outros pulsando a vida.
Esperando não existe relação pra acabar dentro do meu coração.
Esperando, penso nas suas piadas, na sua voz expressiva e nos seus braços ajudando a preparar churrasco.
Esperando, abraço a sua lembrança e com ela sigo administrando lidar com as ilusões dele.
Esperando, você se mostrou um homem que vale esperar pra ter qualquer coisa.

95

Esperando eu entendi que se ele não respeitar meus limites, estou em perigo.
Esperando, tenho medo que essa falta de entendimento do que é permitido acabe em colapso.
Esperando, quero pedir socorro, pra não correr pra Suíça e pedir uma eutanásia.
Esperando pra começar a viver até quando?
Esperando você até quando?
Esperando, seguimos separados
Esperando também me questiono
Esperando o quem?
Esperando chamar o seu nome como se por algum motivo extremamente sobrenatural, você soubesse que estou precisando de abrigo.
Esperando, durmo com a mão na barriga do gato
Esperando, acordo de novo pra ter outro dia te esperando!
Esperando, olho pra lua e a uso como um satelite desejando que todos possam estar felizes em paz.
Esperando, suspiro bem profundo
Esperando a ilusão deixar espaço pro agora.
Esperando muito por mim mesma.
Esperando voltar pra onde sempre encontro você, seja lá o que você seja!

Esperando consciente que essa viagem me guia avante
Esperando aqui estou onde a ilusão não tem pressa pois seria muito pior viver sem ela, tendo enfrentar a seco a total ausência de esperança de um dia derreter ao seu lado ouvindo a trilha sonora da espera.

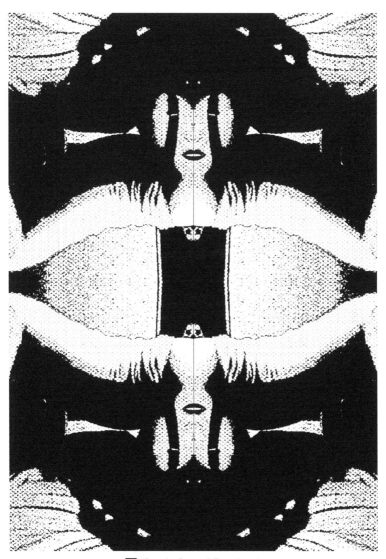

 "Breathe Deeper" Tame Impala.

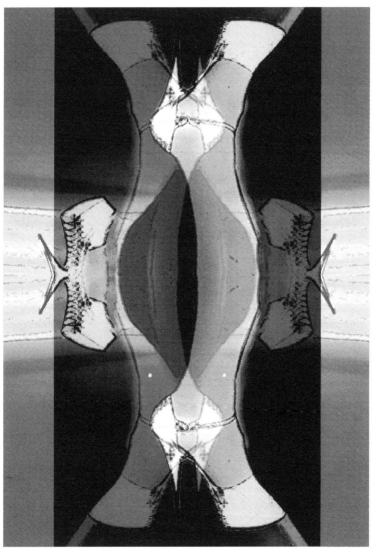

"Tango - Eduardo Castillo Voodoo Remix" Luca Bacchetti.

CROSSED SEAS
MAKE MOVIES
TAKE SHOTS
ALCOHOL AND IMAGES
WRITE SONGS
WRITE BOOKS
INTERNAL DIALOGUES
TO EXPLAIN ALL THIS

WILL YOU EVER LISTEN?
WILL YOU EVER MAKE A MOVE
MY MOVIE TO YOUR MOVE
MOVE! TIC TAC TIC TAC
THE WAY YOU WANT IS HERE
HAPPENING NOW!

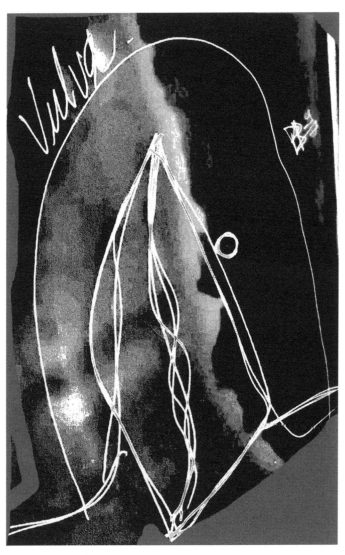

■ "Late Night - SOLOMUN Remix" Foals.

100

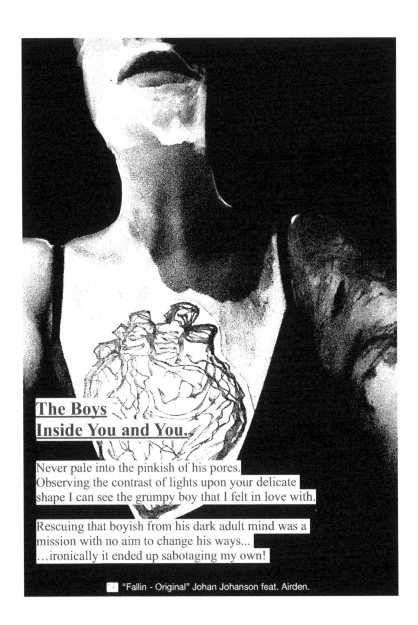

The Boys
Inside You and You.

Never pale into the pinkish of his pores.
Observing the contrast of lights upon your delicate
shape I can see the grumpy boy that I felt in love with.

Rescuing that boyish from his dark adult mind was a
mission with no aim to change his ways...
...ironically it ended up sabotaging my own!

"Fallin - Original" Johan Johanson feat. Airden.

101

One side of this cold bed was maintained with a lot of emotions running strongly, against the eminent emptiness of the touch. The other sides... I have no clue.

A little adjustment would do, archiving forever until it lasts. Both blind driving each other mad for the sake of 8 seconds of regrettable glories.

I'm still alone talking to my mirrors night after night.
Why do I feel good on my own? What is this guilty in my pleasurable moments with myself and I?
If I was not me, I would pick to be myself!
Why does the voice coming from within says that I don't need any of these stupid puzzles? Silence.
My sins are far way lighter, than the burden of being your best shot.

In our space, verbalising my thoughts was never a problem until I realised it doesn't mean you want to be part of it. No one between us, really wants to work things out tactically.

Is all this rubbish about porn and sex addictions?
Is it all about trust but don't trust to trust deeper again?
Is this healing your past?
Whatever rings true, the lack of getting out of your shell to embrace the sun is holding back your future!!
My social skills are naked in a pond, waving for you to come close to turn the tango on.

■ "2203" RDF.

Ignoring the pages tinted blue, bring back those pretty smiles that I normally burst, when any of my cats, meet me in casual laughs. I am the jumpstart of your serotonin. We sing the same songs and we like it dark. The clouds will open up again at some point, changing the direction.

I was there.
The grumpy boy locked me in his world for 2 sevens! Melted my heart so many times, just welcoming the sincere smiles once the textures of the fabrics, cuddled the pinkishness of his satin skin.

It was for the love of something so much bigger than a dark romance. Kinky is glowing from the sun of our winks. I respect the delight even if I can not share the same enthusiastic clap coming from your eyelashes.

It's for art. The art which set us all free. Art explaining for you, me and him... We are all in a karmic circle.

I love you and him, you love me, he loves everybody. Many people seem to be in a similar kind of madness. Everybody loves everybody, (as long they don't get too close), right?! I don't get it! Where is my return for so much well-invested attention?

Hearts switching positions on a confessed triangle of friends. She asked to her fella, in order to bring peace of mind and clarity for this love charade:

"How many lines are needed to make it even more clearer?"

■ "Come Close To Me" Romare.

103

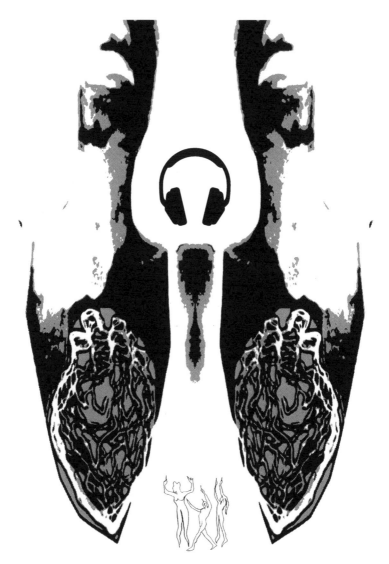

"Global Grove" Squid & Cosey Fanni Tutti.

Living so long as part of a game that only reveals what got behind the door ages after I crossed the entrance.

The void singing tuned in our dirge, walking side by side, aiming in different directions of our desires. Love merged with resentment of everything that could be, but never was.

It's never to be a sonnet in the carnival of traumas and selfishness. The way you see me, against the way I see you, colliding with the frustrating reality that we want more because we became somebody else.

I'm probably losing here not only my patience, but interest. Why bother if I'm a solo queen, watching with eyes wide open, another pair of eyes rolling up frozen by alcohol and middle-class drugs.

So far so close, so similar, especially at the wrong timing, it makes me think about jumping out of this boat! There is a lot of life out there, where my winkles can shine absolutely divine. All are available without apologising.

Reality is here; my place is to observe and studying ones' mind; I learn about the acceptance of the natural variation of the human brain. He is on a spectrum in behaviour patterns, and I am married to him.

I forgot how to have a relationship where one pretend to be a prey. Heterosexual frisky from the 90s, where a kind of approach, with information, can be seen as a way of violation of personal space. An uncertain taste, inappropriately touching another person's emotions. Quiet breaths pays out faster than a full blows.

"The Night Watch" Tor Lundvall.

Boy.."Boys boys boys" I always appreciated you, being older than me. Now in my 40s, the rush to prove my genuine intention of moving on, has been very time-consuming.

I have to ask myself, compared to the offered (despicable) returns. Oh, how am I not yet, studying anthropology?

This quote and valses, from the floppy fellas convention are boring me now. Everything takes ages!. Inhibited sexual desire for the many lucky bastards to the unbreakable 5 against 1 game. Fast food and porn? …and that's what 2020 you turned to be. It's not another constructed paradigm of monogamy written here. I think 5 fingers against your kinky, give us the wrong mono action between, what was meant to be, us, a duo! Me and you! Capice? Capice my arse!! My beautiful arse!!

If I will see the sunshine once again in another port, don't be so surprised. You got your hand, to cuddle you at night.

To someone else, I could say, I'll not be surprised by my own future; when the time comes to life, my pipe will be dry, by the delay of your response. Said that, I put my arm in the air, understanding that a weak mind, should never come close to me. For that reason, I respect you a lot.

So many styles, so many drinks for one! Breakfast for one... Even if our illusion lives under my skin, I'm in love only with myself. My ideas shift into this private club noir of me, and since I have no plans to stay forever crying it out, tell me how to get you back, to the desirable wine walls.

We all got to get a grip! (*whoever this line applied to, considering possible hidden eyes in the dark, decaying the adult, which Cindy, me and you tried to portray*)!

■ "All Too Soon" Trentmoller & Lisbet Fritze.

"Dan Solo" Groove Armada.

Strong Guys and Mr Dickhead

Her views of encounters regardless of time.
Everything already happened
but also not so soon.
The way I heard it, from now translated,
getting as accurate as possible.
I will keep it in the first person.

The way I promised to my dearest deep friend.
Confessions from minds to the mirrors.
All those habitants inside my atoms, understand the
reason for such an elaborate chessboard of an
introduction.
Past present and forever that is still to become true?
Think! When you wake up, I will be there!

All the happenings, before that morning, it was never
too late. The first strike of my pose. Only my breasts
were exposed. Sitting on his lap, already soaking.
The way to describe those lips is tricky. Think about
a man who really enjoys sucking your breasts for
days! Equally amazing is my attractiveness to his
persona. He knows I like it.

He had drugs enough for a week, but the afternoon
faded into a research for the best high, for our best
night. All written like it should be, soon after
breaking the silence.

"Strong Island" JVC Force.

We spent 24 hours sniffing, kissing and getting comfortable with each other. We slept for so many hours, a solid rest for the mind. I felt protected.

The sounds of the waves were acting like a clock. He woke me up sucked my breasts again, and said a few things to make me laugh. In a second, I kissed his proud and strong fella. Pillow talk and the waves.
He says to hold the stories, all in, with my cottonmouth.

Avocado for breakfast, the perfect crystal bread, brie and strong Manuka honey. The mobile phone showed 10 calls, from a mega drunk friend, catching up with my attention, to the time and space. Let's keep the day on a good vibe
(I thought)!

Sounds of the windy seaside of the Kent coast!
We don't have to go anywhere, but his mate wants to know what happened to us. He met us in their local pub a few days before.

The guy knocked on the door bringing a cat in his hands. The poor thing was not well. Seems a seagull has a fight for a bit of steak, which the cat didn't hold well. Hard to believe, but the seagull down there are bad asses.

While I was looking after the little cat, his mate was staring at me for ages, saying, *"yeah, now I see why he doesn't want to meet other women."*
What an unusual thing to say I thought!
"Is this a scene plotted by both of you?" I said in a jokiest way.

"*Hey, trouble! I would never spend time training a seagull, to attack a lost kitten, hoping my timing could be right, to have you deliciously, with your messy hair, in my kitchen, ready to listen to my mouthy friend saying that yes, I'm not interested in any other person! Well to be more honest, I asked him to come here, to tell you that, but the Seagull and our new cat were really unexpected!*" Exploding, laughing, and a bit of a sniffing in, whatever he had left upper his nose.

His elaborate ways of saying things to me really turn me on. That was a very straight forward "Joke no joke" from him... which, I secretly pray to be true!

We were all laughing and I didn't really know what was going on. A second, but loud, knock on the door.

The police were over-friendly, but eagle-eyed in everything we were saying. They were there with a mad woman. She was in her pyjamas shouting that her little kitten was stolen by that "Mr Dickhead". She Pointed to my boyfriend's mate!

The police didn't get inside the house. Everything was explained about how "Mr Dickhead" took the kitten away, just to avoid being bitten to death by the seagull.

The woman said, "*You are a dickhead! A seagull was not beating my kitten" that was our family duck!*" Letting out that apparently, Mr Dickhead only got the wrong bird. He is the kind that only gets the wrong birds anyway!

■ "Hand On The Pump - DJ MUGGS remix" Cypress Hill.

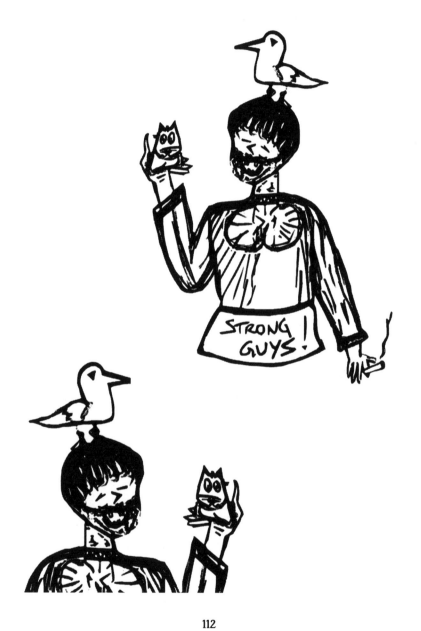

The last one of his catches, was Lacy, who applied fire to burn the seat of his car, in a jealous attack, in front of his grand parent's house. Yeah! Some people are hardcore drama in England!

Very cliquey atmosphere; we just want the police away. Fuck this nonsenses, the cat was safe, but the drugs on his bed were making me almost to faint. It was only for us to have fun together, but as a coward as a chicken, I can say that I am too prude for crime! I am too nerdy for that! I have to feel safe!

All things were explained and after all the thanks and goodbyes everybody was in a huge hit for a line.
Hours talking the same over each other's laughs, then "Mr Dickhead" said:
"*I have some "strong guys" for a good rough naughty round, if you guys fancy.*"

The look on my face was the old "What are you talking about?" and I said *"What exactly are the "Strong guys?"*
"The only strong Guy here is my patience to have you around dick head!" Said my fella cutting any possibility of bullshit to come out from Mr Dickhead's mouth.

Mrs Dickhead, placed his crystals on the table and said to us that he was happy if he could just be there quietly watching us getting together because he was feeling lonely! *"I don't think I could handle her, anyway!"* that was the last of dickheads' words!

■ "Dog in Heat (feat Redman & Method Man) Missy Elliott.

I looked at my partner in that crime and I made him understand that I was not comfortable with that situation (even if his friend was attractive, his personality was so repulsive, he would not even do for a wank, in the dark, crying! What a wally! Funny, but not funny like sad funny. *''No, No, NO, you are tripping, mate!''* After that, he was invited to leave the building.

Another two days of fun and promises for the recovery of the fits. After a walk on the beach, basically it was new to many winters wearing different colours of fresh pillows. Apparently, his friend was always inconvenient and he is still offering the "strong guys" to couples around.

The best we can do is to give ourselves
some peace of mind, a spliff to listen the
sounds of the waves. Our nonsense
hair cuts. All the stars smiling
to us together with
the brightest of all,
the killing moon.

"Tunic (Song For Karen)" Sonic Youth.

 "Noir Désir" Vive La Fête.

The blink which helped no teeth to smile.

Once Upon a Time, in another galaxy, while I was working as a resident DJ for a posh club/terrace, I saw a lot of things, and aspart of the odes, I received unusual gifts from time to time.

The secret (never verbalised by me to any human on this planet) and The story of a Cartier necklace.

Between many stories banging on my door, one of them had a twist that, until this day sleeps in my past. It reminded me of an utopian situation that happened in this realm. For as long as I can remember, it seems this is the only thing I never told anyone about it.

Try to picture it. He was always by himself drinking whisky. Tall and very clean cut, I just remember him always dedicating a bottle of champagne for me, smiling very elegantly, and not showing too much enthusiasm towards the rhythm.
Once the bubbles were presented to me, the way he asked the barman, to attach a beautiful red satin ribbon, only to my glass. The barman was well tipped, to focus on the right glass, which should have been given to me.
A very important detail about tipping the barman right, when you ask for some kind of favour. Kids, never forget, always tip the bartenders! They are the pulse of our night life. Take my advice to your heart and always treat bar staff with respect!

Every time somebody dedicates a bottle of champs, I always share it with the people working in the place.
It's always a very special gift offered by those who can afford and understand the intentions behind my tunes.
Very powerful sounds, sensual, but extremely elegant and sometimes political. Many times an ode for a big personality. Music nonstop!

The red ribbon man took my attention NOT because of his generosity or looks... honestly I vaguely remember his face!

I was tipsy and that night was so packed. After a DJ set, I went out for a ciggy, in a quiet corner outside the club.
He was at the door, talking to the owner of the club.
I ended up talking to them. My boss said I was his "Golden ticket to have so many beautiful people dancing until 7:00 a.m."

My boss was a prick type and he only could be half friendly with me, all because I was "*too large for his frame.*" I remember just replying, "*I'm glad I'm too large for your frame because I have no interest in your little man's traumas.*" I genuinely said that and we became half friends; once the other half, was my boss.

The red ribbon man said "*she is the reason why I get so drunk every time I'm in this country until I forget her.*" Saying that in a very boyishly way.
Laughing, but glad about the joke, I said, what about the ribbon?
He very elegantly said to my boss, "*I'll see you tomorrow. Now I'd like to ask about a song, that your DJ played earlier in the evening.*" Walking away from my boss with a Red-ribbon's hand behind my back, he winked showing off his confidence.
We walked a distance to give us a bit of privacy, while he was telling me about, how my boss was his mate at the bank they worked in before. "Do *you work in a bank?*" I asked.
He said he was sometimes embarrassed to say he worked in a bank because he was not "*That kind of bank man*".
Ok, I couldn't give a damn if he worked at a bank or in a bar, to be honest. I was intrigued by the red ribbons only on my glass.
The symbology behind that gesture, was feeding my curiosity to a level stronger than my social skills. I said, " W*hat about the ribbon*"? He said…" *Two red ribbons! I think the first was a year ago*" He continued talking to me, very calmly like in a Jim Jarmusch black and white movie. "*Your energy just connects me with music. Electrifying to be around you; I have been watching you DJing for a sometime while. You are always singing your tracks. I bought those ribbons in Japan. They were made to adorn some special parts.*" The man was good with his words!

Young and free!
Hours late, waking up at his amazing place, he showed me photos he took secretly while I was DJing.

■ "Etre Assis Uu Danser" Liaisons Dangereuses.

He told me he was going to get married to an old friend from the family business. His future wife was a model from overseas and she was not interested in men.

Four nights are spent listening to amazing music while drinking sparkling water and lemon and some exotic tea from the Himalayas. Smoking the frequency of his momentum of being himself, I understood he was not there to make friends. Once, he chef-prepared a French new cuisine, which was a disaster because he could't cook at all; We decided to go for a Burger at "Burdog da Dr. Arnaldo" Ah, I wish to tell more if I just could remember more! It was so much more than these. He was around, on and off, between months of never remembering his last goodbye. We were always so stoned, "The joy of youth!"

We liked to have a few nights, sometimes in hotels normally after an after-party, where he would confess how he had been hunting me down through the night. The truth of his words was lost in time for sure. My routine was to work at many parties and always be introduced to new people, all smiling around town. It was absolutely amazing times!

Our last encounter happened a few weeks before his upcoming marriage somewhere in the pacific. DJ
He was very stressed and we spent a night sniffing with people calling his phone all the time. It was his goodbye and his chosen stag do was with me.

In an unusual burst of emotions, he threw his phone against the wall. *"I had enough of these people"* whatever those people were! He broke a glass just out of being clumsy.
After stopping me from collecting the glass from the floor, he kissed me and said, *"Come on, let's go else where…where I'll be only with you."* Here we go, I had no idea where!

Driving his car was very relaxing, contrasting the outbursts from the last hour. He was telling me about how he never felt so free as when I was around.

Named a thousand dances and heavy parties, he never was appreciated for his fun artistic appreciator side. It was always only about how handsome and rich his title was. The mad thing was, I didn't even know his name! I was so embarrassed to ask his name. I used to call him the "Red Ribbon".

I do still not knowing today and if I combine that with the fact, that even the image of his face, is blurish, it fades in my memory.

He can be any man with an amazing Swiss Cottage in his early 50s, married with to face with a view, kids, all in a beautiful portrait placed on a fireplace! I just wonder if he is still reading about Thelema and Kabbalah.

I was so high! The conversations were like minds in heaven! Oh, and the performance of that Krav Maga man was the most moistest!

We got to a massive gate. The lift was so exclusive that he needed a passcode to his car to be lifted to his absolutely beautiful, messy mansion in the sky.

The unfamiliar territory of wealth in a foreign language, overviewing the lights of my dark and wet city.

The images on the walls were fabulous. He had one of my sketches framed and placed, close by a huge Italian sculpture in the shape of a round female figure, with lights coming from a hole.

Non stop talking, he came with a very distinguish box. We made ourselves comfortable then he showed me, an amazing necklace. That was one of his future wife's wedding presents. Accordantly to his words, he bought that thinking of me.

Even the box was a serious piece of statement.
He said… "Can you please wear it for me?"

I was petrified in fear by the responsibility to have to handling that piece of art, being as tipsy as I was. Too much!

"Oh my God. It's probably worth a fortune! I really don't want to touch it, not even the box I want to touch!" I said that laughing, but I was slightly embarrassed by my lack of sophistication.

"Like A Bad Girl Should" The Cramps.

He said. "*The box is just silly! Come on, they all end up inside another box anyway!*" Well, that was probably a joke, that only super-rich people can get it.

He firmly insisted and 22 hours later, we were singing, both super drunk, just wearing the necklace and ribbons made out of one of his ties.
We dressed his sculptures and also we had a fashion run away, just applying the only garment to my body that amazing Cartier Necklace! The one is the cat! "*A Panther, for a laugh!*".
He was very into my shapes, tasting waters because I had some deep south Richard Kern, on a DVD, a pinch of weird.

We wrote things around the walls of his place; he filmed himself writing something in a foreign language.
Another day only for trip-hop vibes, that he freshly had bought back from Bristol. No promises of tomorrow just right here and now. We were miles apart by our class division, but so close to be enjoying those moments of feeling free.

He had bespoken produced drugs, accordingly with his body metabolism. It was all very surreal for a working-class young adult like me! Dutch and fun, like his orange sofa, I felt something like Amsterdam on velvet nights!

The naked karaoke with frozen sake, until getting lost in translation. Vaguely remember both of us reading a sort of pagan spell to increase the power of gratitudes and grace! We thought we were into witchcraft, at some point!
Also we had some form of deep conversation about fear of the next fall! What a trip! Life is good! No long-term expectations, just a few nights of intense fun.

Blessed we were and we always will be, according to his words! We went to a breakfast with booze and two cabs. One for me to go back home and one for him, towards his future.

A few weeks later, it was his wedding day, somewhere miles and seas away from where I was.

A cold Thursday night would not really be memorable for me; I wasn't thinking about him at all. He was a very special encounter that I knew would be impractical to trip on any type of imaginary commitments. I didn't even liked his fashion anyway! Oh, God, it makes me laugh now; after everything I lived after those nights, his fashion was far more classy than I could understand. I was in love with my work; I loved to be a promoter and DJ. There was no space for a new platonic love, and if I recall well, it probably was a chair already occupied by someone else, as impractical as the wealth mad man.

On that cold night, I received a bottle of a special champs with an edible gold chocolate card. It came in a beautiful craft cardboard box, with a card written *"This gift is for you to remember when we were walking like panthers that night!"*. The chocolate card was a special piece of edible art.*"If you don't eat you don't make the magic happen"*. Ah, It blew my mind!

I was fascinated by the theatre behind his "Oferenda" to me. The action of understanding the small details of something full of meaning. An edible treat like our encounters, very fast to swallow and unique. I'm not sure about what I tried to express in the last sentence. Fast to swallow? I'll keep, "Just because"!

That "Champs" I didn't share with my working colleagues. This was the first and only champs he dedicated to me without a special glass! Felt something was missing but, that was the first champs given without him there.
Maybe he forgot about tipping the bartender.

Ironically enough "The man with no teeth" (*that's how the gentleman, who was in charge of the cleaning of the club, was usually to present himself, he loved the funny aspected of his fake teeth*) asked me if he could take the boxes from the gifts away or if I wanted to keep them.
He said something like, *"There are chains, pieces of paper and some broken glasses. Do you want them?"*

126

I didn't even check it. I was so mesmerised by the edible card! The whole meaning of that gift was the message on the bottle! I really didn't even look properly inside the box. From a distance, I dedicated my drink to sending my sincere thoughts of happiness, using with my music to get close to those celebrations so far from me. The joy of having lived those hunting moons. It was easy to setting myself free from having any hopes of seeing him again.

Years later, I heard a story of a cleaner, who worked at the same club as me. Seems he found a chain with a cat in the middle of the bar's rubbish. It was around a broken glass inside a box. A case of negligence from the bartender or perhaps, somebody forgot to tip the bartender!!!!

Yes! "The man with no teeth" sold a Cartier necklace probably for its weight in gold; God knows what happened! He not only could afford a new set of fake teeth for himself and his misses but also he paid for his son's drug debts and rehabilitation.

Fragments of my past, where a Cartier-red-ribbon-krav-maga-golden-chocolate-mad-man, gave teeth to no tooth! I kept it as a secret that I never spoke about it because nobody would believe it, in the first place. Fantastic things happened in your life, right? Thats the way the band sounds to us all.

"Red Ribbon" I don't know what or where you are now. I don't know your name or face. I could only say, please, please, please be happy like the way I remember you writing on your own walls.

At last "The man with no tooth" could walk smiling like a panther for many nights!

Arigato money!
For you and me.

"Let Me Be Me" The Other People Place.

"Orange Romeda" Boards of Canada.

"U Can Dance" Bryan Ferry & DJ Hell.

The trip to light

The point with no return, sealed by songs and solo pagan rituals. Under the predictable abundance of light, in high latitude climates two. From noon until noon again.
Ah, Please be real! Summer vibes into the unknown.
Since the first flame erupted, every song was written about us.

The movie of our lives is not always in harmony with time and space. Never planned all this to end up to be a certain type of 12 steps for you.

Your experiences skipping in the shadows, all misled, very suddenly since the future became alive.
Hold my hand and teach me what is missing inside you.
My mission is on the way to completion; once more, the beat mixing is fresh from the heartbeat. I could count the days, hours and seconds to the new gig but I'm in love with getting immersed in words and memories.

On the beach, awaiting for the city to come undone and then, at some point, Jupiter will put his coat, on Venus' shoulders at night. Mercury wears the Pluto's helmet, Orcus, but can you see throw the darkness?

The channel to the stars after the breaking free from different chains and prisons. A story was written on walls and paper, giving me shelter under your silence, since my pages were whispering the little mysteries of us all.

You could be me, you, him, us or them

Drawings of my deep desire to justify my attitudes.
Don't worry; If we get what we gave, so we both have a thousand lives to use them in happiness.

Evolution breaks old dogmas since you never knocked on the door. Never asked anything even if there was something between us anyway.
Is this seat a better place than the action and motion? Ha!
I don't know what is on your side of the river. I can only wish you well while translating that song singing our dreams. The extracted words could make me feel that I belong here now, more than ever.

> *"My best friend, whatever happens*
> *I'll swallow tears and breathe in your hair*
> *Misbehaving, we cry in each other's embrace*
> *When we meet*
> *When we kiss"*

Come leaning closer as the tale unfolds to stop living high and dry. My senses went through every emotion known to man. Exchanging imaginary comas, basically ransacking thoughts, eager to get some attention. Realise now that the reader has no interest in my cause! I gave it out, too much, too young. The reader doesn't know what has been trading in this den.

How crafty a situation can be locked in its own box.
My attitudes are just portraying myself and my intentions poorly, with no chance to refine the words over a drink.
Advocating against my will, I was jumping into the fire, ignoring the fact that I didn't even want anything serious!

Bored by repetition while hiding a sore throat. You were never close, specially after I undisguised, sang to you all about broken hearts. Feels like constantly climbing to hit the top of a melting iceberg. It never gets to the top!

Where is the opportunity to find my blinking lazy state of noise and fun inside him? Intense, but so distant. We could get on like a house on fire, but the eight o'clock news never will be about us.

The empty wallet of broken promises is open. Loved so many as fast as we forgot them. Kicking progress to move forward with my happy future. Senseless written under silence. A mixed cloud of informations coming to British homes, and also from overseas hearts and smiles.

Cindy, around the Sun, showed everything she could do in her power. Inside out, her thoughts waved for practical solutions. She is not into cosmology, but into moneylogy!

Since collected narratives never took place, here comes a conclusion. The devil pointed out that the problem is not to have illusions, but what you do with them.

Don't act like the other side has any responsibility for your emotions because it is just an illusion. No action is required! This game aims to become someone I want to live with.

I'm getting by, leaving you and me behind. My mind is rescuing the sun after the thunders. I'm through with this sensation washed up. Focus on the greens welcoming a new spring and summer. Time will tell how we bang those drums.

■■ "Year Of Silence" Crystal Castles.

Two six nine eight anxiety

Our
TWELFTH
most common
element...
TO TASTE LIKE FEAR!

SATURATED by a
lo-fi handheld
HEART!

Sensory overload or
Heavy-gauge sheets.
NEUROTOXICS
NEVER RUST my electrical
conductor!

x2
x2
x2
x3
x16
x3

Bloom and Fade
Three genders of aluminium
Apollo turned around the face
Zeus took pity on them,
Trying to put a spell on me.

I tried to be the lover of the hard-working man
but the Gods of arts never will allow me to have it fully!
Was it all in vain?
Probably, it was in vain for him!
His memories are like shots of dopamine.
Thank you so much.
I have nothing to regret.

On this cold afternoon
An eulogy of Socrates when I was baffled,
taking me to salute the sailer.
I demand all sorrow to be transmuted
to violet lights in the sky.

Cuddling the cat, collecting the records,
then in a blink, life goes by!

Back to reality, I'll gonna go to the land
where my smiles are taken as treats of love
instead of threads of imaginary betrayal.
Aluminium.

■ "Impossible" Royksopp.

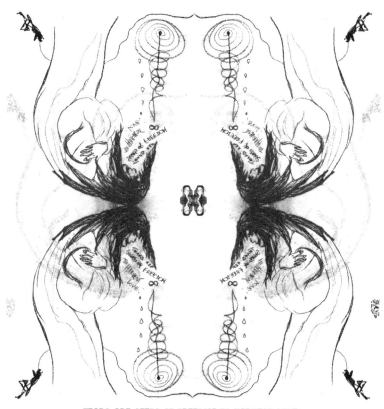

TEARS ARE SEEDS OF FREEDOM TO HARVEST LOVE.

"Superstar" Sonic Youth.

"Fuzz Jam" The Lazy Eyes.

137

"Let's Kiss" Beat Happening.

138

From an old book shop in NYC, a found old letter...
...gave space to enter someone else atemporal mind.
It could be easily just being written by myself.
Dated ''1984''.
No signature, no names; it could be any one.
A few infos were changed just to make it contemporary!

Here it goes:

''*Since our time at school, you were always around me.*
Where words serenely sweet expressed your way to show
attraction even when you pulled my ponytail to call me "fat"
for no reason at all. Your essence touched me many times.
When I think about you, I can close my eyes and all the best of
dark and bright flourished again in my smiles. You are alive
inside people's minds, so I know you will find this letter at
some point. The clue was spiking on our skin when you wanted
to hold me that night.

No matter what you fancy in the morning, there is always only
one truth when you close your eyes.
You said, "Let us roll all our strength, and sweetness up to a
big ball."

You have been sleeping with beautiful sisters (a must to be able
to enjoy my company fully). You have it all, the looks, the
elegance, the surname, the smile, the power, the money, the
body, the charisma ... Name yourself what is missing!
My love couldn't cope with your abstinence of words.
I hope you can forgive me, but I can no longer wait.

Painfully I watched myself saying, NO, Thanks!
Carpe Diem.''

––––––––––––

Take the plunge

Last night a song was telling me about the awareness of how dark the next mirrors can be even after I had enough about the lows.

What an amazing journey! I've been fabulous, even drowned in tears! Nobody knew that my powerful glow and grooves also cohabit with my teen spirit persona! Repeat after me, "I am not driven by sorrow, but by laugh and passion."

Working on the recent disgrace to clean the sins out of the craving, proving to myself from the past, that a comfortable present is just a question of time... it worked!

"Like A Stone - Live Version" Audioslave.

A change from the devil I know for another that I dedicate my daily 8 seconds of flux. Petrified by my lack of sense. The black swan is lost in his own blindness to my light on the horizon.
How to dance on this surface and to write about the sunshine?

Yeah! Go on then, don't talk! Don't tell me about that funny joke and how blue the sky was yesterday! Oh Boy! I wish, boy!
It will never be easy, but bite me, drink me, mark me... and I'll gently whisper your name cause there is no land to return.

I ate the lotus and in the dark, yours I became. I'll Attribute that to the down side of long-term belonging to nowhere near the north.
Don't surrender easily, but keep me fed with illusions.
I am too much happiness to take, for someone so stubborn like you.
Let's wait another 7 years, then maybe I will be telling you all the adventures I didn't have the opportunity to live with you one day. All blame is on still life to disguise my impotence in acting upon the inevitable. The bill is mine, I know. Once I was wearing myself down covered in yesterday's illusions. A spirit was in decline.

In the light, we see the direction of the next port. Two worlds and in between your river and my seas. Hot sun to park my mental anchor next to the right sounds, which once, we believe could be in your light house. The silver surfer sapio-sexual keeps me true from within.
I'm still waiting for that knock, taking me from the point you once silently left. How present are you in my realm? Not enough yet! Never enough?
Take The Plunge, baby!
Otherwise, if I can make you so, then I break you too.

■ "The Same Deep Water As You" The Cure.

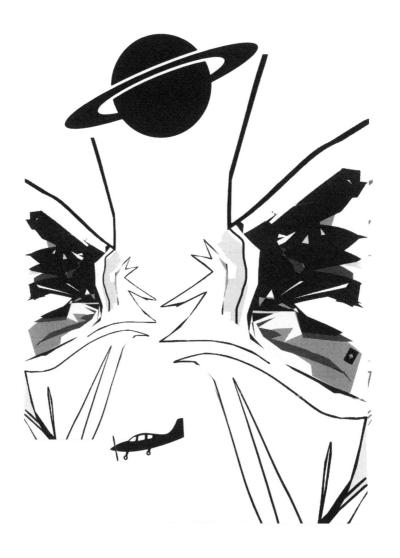

"Cabin crew, prepare to take-off"

Seat number 1F.
Heart in a groove safer than down there on those dirty streets.
Snakes to the ground when I am turning around in the skies.
Over the skin of his silk rests the scars that I badly want to forget. Double daring myself to fly away from the pain. We look hard to see for real, but I wanna see you come back as the light. That light over there, which seems resting so tiny, from blessed clouds.
I wrote two books up here and much more.
My time inside airplanes is trying to learn from Raymond Pettibon's style. Words, drawing shapes and people passing by. A place where I find peace of mind. Perhaps always a little more connected with the clouds than I would like.

I usually plan the trip for days by organising my luggage; I really got homesick, previously going anywhere. Once I am at the airport, then I am in full power to have fun!
To Ibiza, I don't plan anything, not even my bags. It's like jumping on a bus to go to an office or something.

Every day, it's important that I feel comfortable, regardless of feeling dizzy, when trying to sail into break your deep water.
To dive under, fascinates me, perhaps more than the stars, but I feel at home in the cosmos. The highs and lights are the places to be recognised and appreciated the way I am.

Hair against the soft wind. On the beach, my office. Urban girl toasted on the sand, basking my uncomfortable true until a song reminded me that I'll always be the bright night in your sky.

There I designed a world. Sometimes I cried and many times I laughed and danced. A few times had sex on the sands, but nothing unforgettable or epic. (A bit shit really!)

I have always loved the sun with the though I am the daughter of the night.
The moon always calls me; she stays up there looking at me and with her glow she asked:
"How long are you going to stay inside the box?"

Aiming to the same bright light I walked in the woods then climbed a few mountains, just to observe what I could only see from the top, guided by the moonlight shadow.

I participated and performed musical rituals in white mountains of marble and noble stones. Magnetic powers of nature for sure! Moon parties with poetry, wine, fire shots and recitations. Never forget the scent of the night when DJing on a beach in Italy.

I was fascinated by the medieval simplicity of picturesque forgotten places in the middle of France.
I educated myself and still learn about the efficiency in Germany. In another life, I've been through "kinos", driving from south to north of Deutschland.

The tiny chocolate cakes in Switzerland and those apples strudels in Austria. All the summer suns and sins, from Saint George's land and the bucolic gardens of England.

Familiar sensations of cool, coming from the pollution of a cold city, where the rain is acidic and smells like a fight.
São Paulo was like a deep love, that doesn't fit in the chest, but unfortunately, it also has the bitter after taste since; It stabbed me dry and cold.

The political madness of an entire nation makes me occasionally angry.
I hated seeing the population suffering and being as cowardly as I am, in terms of social mobilisation, the best way to run the world was to run my own.
I'd never be happy living in the middle of social injustices there. In 2000 nobody was in the mood to protest.

Being on an airplane was the realisation of everything I wanted. I can say to be able/free to travel is my greatest accomplishment.

I understand my own memories, when I learn from a new culture. Exploring places helps to forgive the city where I was born and left. Sao Paulo you are mad. I love you and like I did, I hope that one day you will forgive me too.
Never it will be forgotten!
That won't be possible and I don't want to.
You are a wonderful work that I never managed to conquer.
In a way, everyone is forgotten on that stone jungle.
My heart like yours is a rock that pulses life.

Projector, I've always been a promoter. Now I move my ideas to my own personal file. Thinking is amazing and allowing yourself to exchange ideas is an absolute luxury.

Let's see the planet without morally biased lenses, so answers for a few issues, might come into light. Fast as a flesh, everything comes to an end. Time to prepare to get there and relax.

I will never have a fixed idea of anything other than creating the mental comfort of being able to change my mind. Redundancies or grammatical errors are out there! I always think of Pythagoras, Isaac (s), Camille Claudel, Plato... and many others.

Threw my worries away as we started to descend to Amsterdam. Mr pilot, who brought us here without turbulence, thank you very much!
The announcement brings my favourite part of the flight:
"Cabin crew, get ready for landing."

So what?
"I think I'm gonna dig myself now."
This last sentence was a reference to Jane's Addiction tune playing on my Ipad.
Final sip on my G&T bag under the seat.
My music is only blasting loud in my mind, coming from my beloved headphones.
Noisemakers with panache, yes, we are!
Aiming to live once again.
To a smoke and a smile.
Air drumming.
Go, summer sun, Go!

———————

■ "The Smoke" The Smile.

MARLYN-WARHOLDING TIME

◼ "Old Skool" Metronomy.

MERLYN-WARHOLDING ME

Miles of waters

She left home at about 03 pm.
Got back the morning after about 07:30 am.
She was wandering around like a zombie.
Day after day, understanding the reasons why life happens the
way it does then there are just untamed conversations left.

She asked my opinion.
I don't drink alcohol if I'm not socialising.
The conclusion passed out sober and groggy by your boredom.
Wonky blues long and tired

Stay strong keeping away the toxic narcissist thoughts
Briefly relapsed with accepted drugs, throwing away sober
objectivity, so in need to operate with this currency.

Miles of waters in a wrong metrical system
Applied in rights of passage, under our bridges.
Blame me here and again, under the moon's eyes.

Observing her paranoias like a plague
My store reflected on the fruit of my loins while the satin was
still here, hurting my flash. A mad snake is piercing the
membrane of my forgotten secrets.

Threatening to go away attacked by my frozen cards.
Sticking together through the hard and good, my face dropped
trying to cope with all their madness.

It's nothing about sex and jealousy, he is the non-typical brain.
Respect and trust are the foundation for any forevers.
Your eyes don't capture my brain waves on the awake of your
disability, which is so hard to conceptualise once being told to.

"The Diamond Sea" Sonic Youth.

You haven't accepted your own darkness
Judging cruel words which was never said by me.
Lines here could be dedicated to all those who are spinning
personal wheels, not clicking my departure.

Malignant oriented narcissist perhaps both of us
Never to become a walking trauma.
My choice is always to choose the light
The shock of the new opening-up
The traces of our truth, to set us all free.

Impulsively I want to say about differences in love
Explained to me about stopping believing in delusions.
I will never be a soul killer bitch, especially when my other
half becomes a son to me.

My story is to be rewritten once again
Focus on seeing this relapse as a restart to something to
learn. The healing of my nations.

Ain't no time for clingy, to be needy or paranoid.
I'll take the hit once again right on my chest.

For now, we are just pleading for this game to turn for good
and the centre of my sun will return. Miles of waters in a
tranquil flux, you should thrive on it.

Outer vision, my right angle cross of consciousness in
strategy to avoid bitterness. All said and done but the truth
is, she only wished to see Arcade Fire together with him.

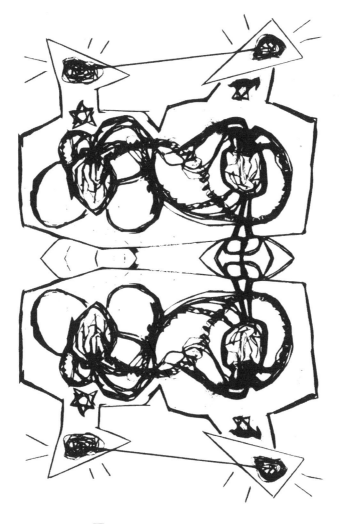

■ "Dance With Me" Nouvelle Vague.

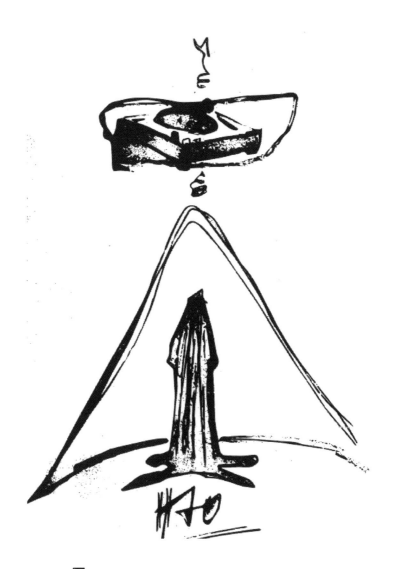

"Come Before Christ and Murder Love" Death In June.

My sacred geometry,

I wish to live in a world where we can focus on practical studies over the conceptualised prejudice toward getting older. I wish a world where the healthy hormonal balance of women is well looked after and taken as a priority for society's development.
Women are natural lovers not fighters!
Genealogy understands other's past.
Open eyes intertwined with the wish to have you here.
My galaxy does not require registration.
Talk to me, invite me. I am listening.
Saint Germain gave me his tools.
Cymatic energy in my 2/4 studies.

Hate to admit this, but if you can not see my light...
...then I might give a change else where!

Ah, If you could have me in your mind
as much as I got you in my lines.
Lines that I could be sharing with you.

Days passing by and the seat still empty and
our sounds are spinning on our devices.

Half session only.
H2O series to Ibiza 2022.

———————————

"Inside Out" Tirzah.

This beat and my body shaking with
Our cliches disguised in pagan sonnets

Praying to the happening to get closer in tune.
Like going into learning to beat mixing.
My reality is truly tailed for a goddess' dream
It can be anything but it is never boring.
Any soul and light from the cosmos are finally watching the way we created the universe known today. Since then, I feel my veins "Trentemøller" and my guts "Groove Armada."
My brain in "The Cure" for you like the vibration breaking our "Avatar." Yes, It is my "Dead Can Dance" time.

Stoned in love with time, these easy words play a part in rebuilding cliches. From time to time, waves of hope, take over those harmed promises of being together.

My Eulogy was the epiphany in the funeral of the chosen one. Many iconic personalities and I was there, as the house worker, in my dark angles, encapsulated with the hype of my high graduation's gear.
Felt like an old-school lecture giving a few verses for the new masters.
Oh, My dear friend! You could see so much further than me! Evolving means so much more than I could visualise.
Now from the Olympia, he observes the fruit of his laughs
"CAUSE I AM A WOMAAAAAAANNN"

Switch sentences to change the subject in parallel.

Always I will be surrounded by others' obsessions with my expressions (normally, it's fine).
Who is trapped to whom?
I am free, but they roll their claws around my invisible gate, stopping my graduation from my own forced mediocrity, to finally be able to smile again, even tasting the fear.

The drips of your sweet will be my prize, which the price I paid in advance, with many spins associated with luck and happiness, in collections of drunk stories. A long "Pixies" drone (as in music), my faith is like climate sounds in chord continuously sounded throughout, all of my day thinking of you. ("The Happening," like drone as in music!)

I wish the same happiness happen to my enemies so they don't think about me. It's so much more pleasurable to rise above the stars when brick by brick was build in those 7 years out of 14.
Kentish waters, will all make 21?
Will we make it at all?

Come together now
Come close to me
Come before Christ and murder love!
Come as you are.
Come fly with me
Come undone
Come dance with me
Love Supreme!
First, Last and Always.
Nice on ice.
Just like heaven!"

How will the cosmos dance to the sound tracks for our happy eulogies? It's up to you.

"Let's Go Dancing - SOLOMUN Remix" Tiga.

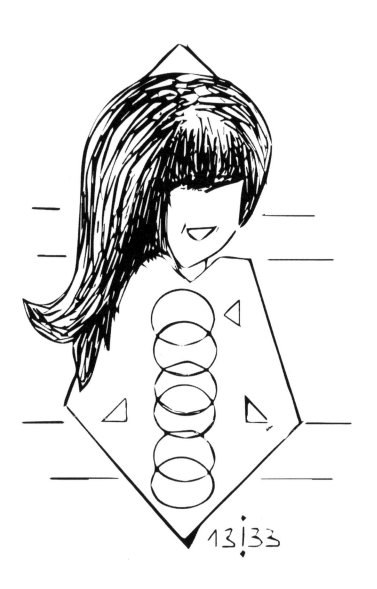

The art work for London Borough of Lewisham's vaccination stories
will be displayed at some point soon.

English couple in Lewisham 2021

THE LIVE SKETCH IN MY BREAK FOR A CUPPA! THE
REALITY OF MY TIME, I SAW HAPPENING WHILE
WORKING AS A VOLUNTEER FOR THE VACCINATION
CREW DURING COVID CRISES in 2021.

"It Was A Very Good Year" Frank Sinatra.

■ "Inside World" WhoMadeWho.

164

Bring the sunset now!

Intrigued by the long silence since he covered his face. Why are you so serious?
Manuscripts of personal codes for a wanted lover.

Their ideology might be similar, leaving a pinch of sarcasm that already took place under bullets of smiles. Their views in politics and science are still greater than all the fuckups, over decades of winning and losing games!

Would you like me more if I project myself more as a loser? Oh, poor me and all that rubbish? I had enough of seeing myself like that!
I am not a victim of my own stupidity, but perhaps I am a little bit self-centered! A small amount of self poison, and the gravity is pushing the dignity down. Hum! Let me get more time time and time just to think about, "Me, myself and I" again...
....cos 44 years seems not be enough of PPRCB.

Telling a story to justify the reason for your shelter. It was once written that a heart can be divided in so many years of anything but nothing and nothings... Achieving the "Nothing at All" bloody status!

Mind talks remind me that emotions are to be felt, but not necessarily long-lasting. The new world is being written from the death of love. People are so empty of hope that illusions are taken over far more than pre-ordered.

I wish I could be as "Serious/no serious" here, as I am on my podcast.

Once I heard that I should want my pants to be tight enough then everyone would want to go to bed with me! It's revolting! His his alcoholic mind does not control his mental way of working out sentences, but to know that does not change how have his illness offended me! Why on earth would I want to everyone wanting to have sex with me? Once he needs a dress to have fun, I reckoned his "Pervert" game doesn't work at all.

Only a fucking imbecile could think that women need to be squashing their canyons, for more offers of sex!

Why does he thinks that anyway?

The middle finger, what for me it's just part of my hand for you it is a deep dark desire! Your untold urges turned into uninvited and brutally forced anthropology studies.

Talking straight to our surroundings.
We all want something so simple.

A few nights ago the sky was so clean that it let me thinking
if one day I would be stargazing again. Laying down on my
kitchen floor, the light bulbs are not as bright or inspirational
as those sparkles out there.
Summer will come sweet, I reckon.

Can I have a wish before pointing the way for a loud
shutting star? Novocaine for my thoughts.

Our chain from this brotherhood might high five out, in big
tens. Arms in the air when we can't help, but surrender to the
beat.

We are made from the same material then be careful with
what we are wish for!
In music, we trust, but will you be there when the sun goes
down?

In sync with our drums, I say to you, just bring your
freshness cos I have the sunset in a bag for two!

■ "Washed Up" Sharktank.

SOMETIMES IT'S WISE TO NOT TALK TO ANYONE
LUCKILY. YOU ALWAYS WILL HAVE YOURSELF.
LIGHTS FROM SELF ANALYSIS.
I WISH YOU A HAPPY NEW YEAR!

"Hot Blooded" New Constellations.

"Save A Prayer" Eagles Of Death Metal.

England

Oh God, I fell for you going down to the den.
How to write about this fabulous light?
The Thames, my friends and this indigo sky.
How warm is home?
The trees and the colour of the grass.
How silly are those who don't love this place?
I see the lines of my face changing here
My spirit is in harmony with all these sacred sounds.
Rainy days watching the silver sea
Even the wind gives us a frozen cuddle
Whispering stories and personal history
In Kent, it was always victory or death.

How honest is our love?
The next chapter is not written yet,
but if you perceive it or not,
It's so well-rehearsed.
How to get a feel of this hidden chemistry?
A sword somewhere between the gardens
and the waves peeping for spells of happiness.
My next exploits are coming with flashes to pose.
I wish to be ready to see you inside,
To ask if there is some mistake,
Since I learnt after the sun and the rhythm.

How just is heaven?
In England, the blues are never emotionally vulnerable.
Even tears have time to drop down,
And even without promises to keep
We don't kiss and tell.
No matter what, never be a grass!
The sophistication of feelings here
Only comes with silence.
The unreal hard knuckles hooligan fights,
When alone/together resting on our thrones,
comes with too many bottoms up in every dawn.

Dreaming with the passion put to use,
Someone cleared his throat in the distance
Hard water marks, we never put the kettle on
and stiff upper lip once again.

I see a fox waiting for the train,
Long gone since I first ignored the rats.
They can live between the dead,
but a foreign heart can not cry anything out.

Every spirit upon freedom remains alive.
Exotic my mind became under your eyes.
Untamed my words about this united perceived kinship
and descent to land and blood. George of Lydda.
A house, a name, a life and an artistic signature.

My tree grew strong in connection with the Avon river.
Cup written in Italian, named a little English star,
adding to our formed art kingdom so far beyond
every predictable expectation. Home, it is here.
My kids & cats, my dreams, love and art,
my sibling and my father's ashes.

Driving at night on my skyline of love,
I heard once that London is a toilet.
Words from jealousy of those who never found,
the streets pavemented with gold.
Only cold faces hidden behind books, the ugly
and we shall not be held liable for any loss of hope.

Here, hey, beautiful England.
How can I forget this good night air?
How to give up the battles?
I just KENT because I love you.

"E-Bow The Letter" R.E.M.

171

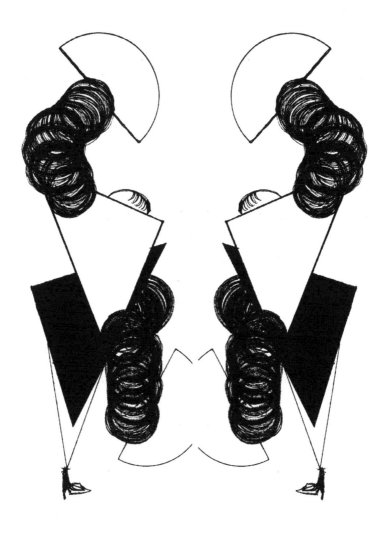

"A Lucid Dreamer" Fontaines D.C.

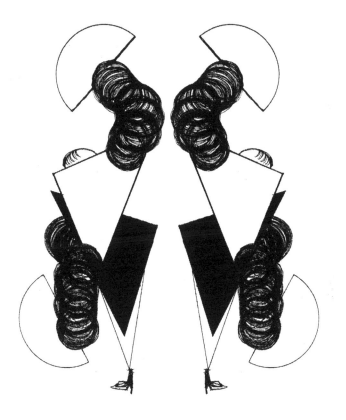

Highly ritualised mating dances drive the evolution of
ornamental combinations of sound, colour, and
behaviour but female preference is incredibly important
in shaping the courtship behaviours of males.

173

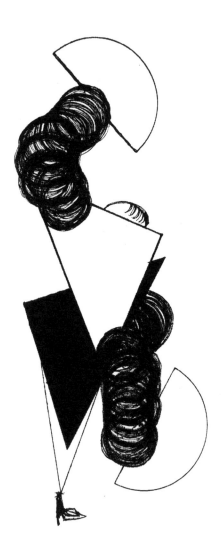

■ "I Know" Autarkic.

Forest fires

I don't wanna be untrue, telling you that I never feel insecure. The windowsill, filled with self-love, doesn't change my mirrors. They are every where here, but we only see, what we want to see. Like every woman on earth, every fairy tale heroine needs a little pushup to bust self-esteem.
The divine feminine pumping up my cells is a force that I did not signed for, as a choice of personality. I was born like this. I don't know how many times I felt inadequate because of it as well.
The reversed adrenaline, thinking I might choose a submarine when the time to sink or swim comes.
Not a yellow one, but a fab, (art deco) submarine!

I don't drink in the winter just to have a few martinis under the sun. Last summer in Brighton, Cindy asked my opinion about her bloke who never reply her messages. He thinks she is too modern (means she "Cagou no pau, Regina!"), probably she was drunk and sent inappropriate messages on WhatsApp once again.

Cindy, darling… *"A confident girl takes no appreciation for misplaced or misunderstood moments of natural dominance. First of all, whatever you have done, you must forgive yourself for being an idiot!"* From that instant I showed her how to talk to the mirror, evoking the powerful woman that is sleeping inside our bellies, saying *"I forgive myself for being such a fucking idiot drinking and then driving him away from me, with my WhatsApp alerts of loneliness thinking about that bastard!"*
We will laugh until 2040 thinking about that moment.

To be "The Man" is a hell of a lot to ask these days!
We need you strong to tame us down! Yeah!

After the fire, she read the following line, using a bottle as a microphone:

175

"Dear b.a.s.t.a.r.d
My lust reservoir was flooding and I was fucking fabulous!
How dare you?
When will the coin drop?
The hardest game you ever came across in your existence is not on yet! Even if you got me hooked to keep this, it requests far more action that will take your mind beyond your dreams and sorrows.

Read us once again; then, you could be in every sentence.
We know I'm far bigger than your mind can handle then all of us together are worth a million times our weight.
You jokily left written a note to mislead our hearts.
Said and done, once someone offered me a castle and I said no. At the end of the night, you clap your hands knowing, from my lips that you will never have anything to regret again.

Want to feel fucking alive?
Become who you were once again, then I could be your prize or price! I wanted to be, but right now, I'm not yours!
I was interested in the soul inside your breath.
This kingdom needs redemption once I should be the only duty call that really matters to you, Batman! Now I want to break free.
I'll be back in the US soon, so give back my gloves and lets call the day for good! Searching for you I met someone new and this new person is me."

Very artistic arms in the air to a dizzy narrative. Cindy decided to call a cab soon after her drunken butterfly performance. I was just observing and collecting data!
"Polly, it's always my boat on your floor vs. his throat under my sole!" She looked at me, with a tear in her eye, saying, " *I just hate to see myself pegging him. It breaks my femininity. He should be fucking me!"* I decided to remain in silence; everybody has some shit to deal with at the moment. We cuddled goodbye, and off she went!
What could I say? Clearly there is no vacancy for the weak left!
It's so much porn stimulating pushing imaginary boundaries at speed far faster than our adaptation to the consequences of this new habits. Only time will tell the horrors and glories.

176

My cells repulse anything that might be used to diminish my pals. Accepting the person's preferences doesn't change our limits. Open up the chat to let the other side to know what your grounds are. Some activities progresses healthier like that and it's vital to work. Why not make your limits clear? She, maybe too late, wrote, "*Refrain from getting close to me if your desire is to make your manhood less of its kind. I got that for breakfast every morning!! Not interested.*" Probably he will have a wank, but she is out.

Post-feminism, individualist we are and we love men.
I could lose my English, for the sake of the comedy of private life! The reality is your browser history, darlings! Broken hearts all the way. What are you going to do about it?
Is our self-esteem problems related to some men losing their masculinity or their desire for us? Re-think it urgently, now!!

Any garments never will hurt me more than to see myself, on the edge to become an oppressor. Oppression never will change what is going on inside our minds. I am not there and if I love him, there is no satin to hurt anymore. Friends we are! I love myself more, and here we are when I accepted the death of my romantic love evolving into something better and bigger. This was written in July 2018. I am over the trauma! Heavy shit, mother fuckers!

To the side on the shadows, who knows nothing about my waters, please accept my wink; I am clearly acknowledging my shame recorded in the past. In a juvenile shot in the dark, when I was in need of kindness. I said it all, too far, too soon. I can only apologise and be grateful for the support. I took the shame!

I think I deserve an extra point for not blaming my Italian blood, catholic education or traditional Brazilian drama queen style! The mountains of strong personality crisis! Once emotions made a house on my profile, the overused "poker face" is not one of my sets of skills and tricks that I possess! Unapologetic, I am exactly what It says on my tin!

It flashes back on that little bistro when I was in Paris with my friend Monica. I remember her calling her man and saying, "*Yeah! Insanely in love with my smell and taste! You will!*" The silence after that sentence, makes me and the next table, to laugh until 2050! Hahaha, for all that madness!

"Look deep in my dark eyes, feel me in, slap me, punishing for our pleasure, your broken mirrors and then fear to say the last goodbye cos you know...I'm not like the other girls!

There is no money that can buy this moments with me. Bastardo" Bastardoooo hahahahaha! Until 2050 rolling on the floor laughing! Her facial expressions, her body language while saying "Bastardo" holding the glass and the wine teeth... Ah, priceless comedy!

My life is always a love story, so here is the reason why I can see those burning forest fires in your eyes.

Cheerio, I'll sail always guided by the light.
To allure our attention by spinning an artistic purse with the anthem for so many of us. We can check the signs then the light flashes the dangerous taste.
That light over there, can you see?
That light, come on!
Said it loud..THAT LIGHT!
That light, in the back of your mind.
That light...That fucking bright light over there
Yes, that cliche, yes!!
The light... The so wanted light,
That never goes out!
X (*as in a new modern way to express in text messages a sound of a blown kiss*).

"Something For The Pain" She Drew The Gun.

"Summer Sun" Cari Cari.

all 📶 🛜   13:07   📶 75% 🔋

X 00:28 ✓✓

No trem
Voltando
Será uma derrota?
Será que estou morrendo
mais uma vez?
Coração no Espeto
Foi
Não é culpa minha
Não é culpa
É entender que o caminho
é esse mesmo.
Estou confortável
Não tem nada que posso
fazer
Aguentar e receber a
bolada no peito.
Estraçalhado um caráter

🙂 📷 🎤

WiFi Call 🛜   13:07   📶 75% 🔋

19

Estraçalhado um caráter
Uma esperança esperando
Nao chegará nunca.
Delete
Bloquei você mesma de
esperar de novo
Nao mereço ser ignorada
Não mereci nem ser
reconhecida
Que merda
Merda.
Querer merda
Desejar estar com um
merda
Ver a merda acontecendo
todos os dias
Respirar essa merda
Esperar
Esperei

+   🙂 📷 🎤

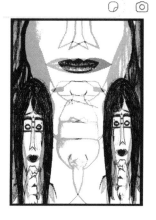

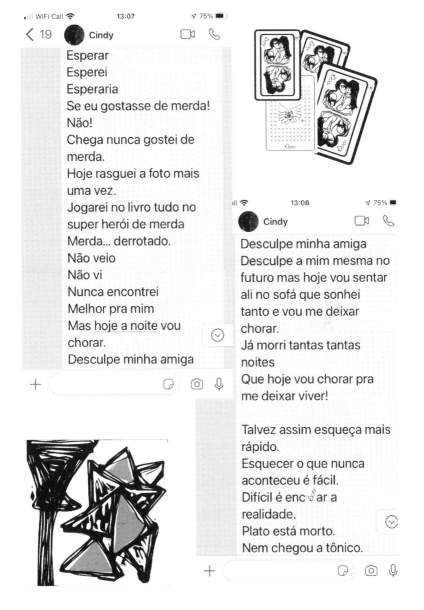

Esperar
Esperei
Esperaria
Se eu gostasse de merda!
Não!
Chega nunca gostei de
merda.
Hoje rasguei a foto mais
uma vez.
Jogarei no livro tudo no
super herói de merda
Merda... derrotado.
Não veio
Não vi
Nunca encontrei
Melhor pra mim
Mas hoje a noite vou
chorar.
Desculpe minha amiga

Cindy 13:08

Desculpe minha amiga
Desculpe a mim mesma no
futuro mas hoje vou sentar
ali no sofá que sonhei
tanto e vou me deixar
chorar.
Já morri tantas tantas
noites
Que hoje vou chorar pra
me deixar viver!

Talvez assim esqueça mais
rápido.
Esquecer o que nunca
aconteceu é fácil.
Difícil é encarar a
realidade.
Plato está morto.
Nem chegou a tônico.

"The Turning Of Our Bones" Arab Strap.

Ain't got no Cadillacs in Catford.

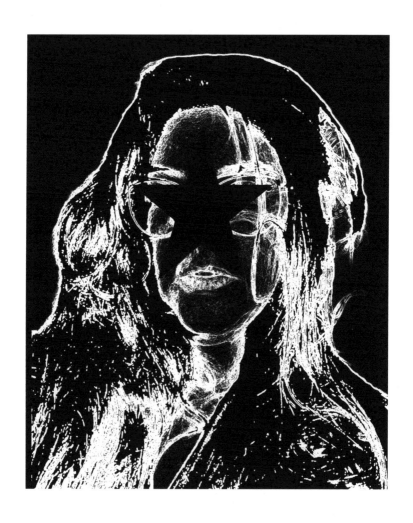

"Lon Bella" Damien Jurado.

My clumsy manners as a carnival queen!

A clown once brought his mate and offered 2 horses to take my sister away with his circus. *"You are my wife now"* style! My opinion was, *"Sister...do you fancy fucking a clown? He once received training to develop his clowning skills, to offer a creepy orgasm!"* That was a terrible joke! I know!

This is a moody morning!
My face is dropping, my heroes are dead, my pocket is empty, I am not traveling as much as I deserve, some of my relatives only talk about plastic surgeries, my teeth are grey and yellow and my procrastination list is getting bigger!
Right, I confess. I like to sleep on my own so I can snore my head off. My lower back doesn't have to hold all the tension between the people panicking around.
Things that make me feel relax?
Let's see... Ah, am I bored enough now?

A glimpse of my past and my ironic self verbalised my thoughts when I am moisturising my face. *"Some lucky people use sperm as a facial cream! I miss those days!"*
In my mind is all about getting together to do something freak with you.

Passively I focus on evoking emotions over things that never happened! Love songs are made of illusions and fuck ups from misunderstandings. Like the moment before the prince turns into a frog or the Goddess who ends up fading into a nightmare of unnecessary questions.

My long-gone Scottish friend. Are you missing my pipe squeezer? Up North the games get hotter, mixed with vodka, meow meow and drums! The sword is the hardest manifest from the beat, in a back-to-back session. Since I choose the other side of the kingdom, I guess in some point, I could return!

My next studies will focus on kundalini, mind frequencies and songs that can deliver higher brain activities to stimulate a stronger climate. I never have an opportunity to try it deeper so its a bucket list sort of thing... Ha! Sexual bucket list! Should I move to the Highlands or to Ibiza?

I am embarrassed to admit that I miss very basic things so badly! Let's talk about facts. Everybody wants to be impressed by the paradise bird. Yeap, dance and dance for me again! I wanna look at the sky at night with no fear. How many years left have you got? Why are we all awaiting to have a life? I can only be there if a full open direct invitation happens.

Venus in Aries learning to be in Libra and the horror of my clumsy manners dancing an indie Macarena! I'm not the paradise bird so this ballet should be only yours!

I really want you to impress me as Burton did to Taylor, but escape any blues. Loyalty and limits well traced saves time and open conversation to visualised the inevitable moving forward.

No shoes in NYC, no boots in Paris and the same bra strongly hold the large bouncy pride. She said destroy and friends we became! He lost her. Seems that nobody really loses someone who doesn't want to be lost in the first place!

Always loyal to those I respect in life. It's healthy to come clean with limits and directions to play the card rights!! Free styling is fashionable for moments of gourmet emptiness. I vote to drive it with sensorial dedication to pleasing all of us!!

My words or grammar might need a large touch of sophistication and I won't apologise for my own utopias! Let me live free of my own ghosts once in a while.

In my mind, he might have a morello cherry flavour, but he is never close enough to inhale his scent.

A warrior, his silence, portrait of a gentleman, for sure! Someone said those who were born to be a soldier never would get to the great commander. I could open a dispute to that paradox.

The real deal can never follow the ideas of a society built by brainwashed people.

Who wants to challenge the dominance skills over someone who was born to be constantly a submission position?

Don't get me wrong, please. The soldier has the power over it all! Generators working for the big picture!

If you think you are an Alpha, think about it again!

We like to exchange dominance for the dominants to upgrade their personal growth. Evolving from whom we were before.

No one is better than me and vice versa. Individual journeys.

We are just a reflection of each other. Stars writing invisible lines, using their reflections drawing the optical illusions on my sky.

In order to be recognised in a placed of dominance, the person has to go to previous releases of own insecurities and naturally to be open, to be called "pig" once in a while! Oiiinc!

I am writing this letter to the unknown. I agree with my internal mind, which plays like a song on repeat, that pulls us together, ironically really tastes like fear!

My musical quotes are not cliches. That's the function of words to pass the message to all of us.

NYC is in my mind.

I wish, I could sing like Patricia Lee Smith.

I am devoted to my mirror and open to learning with your mirrors, all about those reflectors upon our skin. Please love yourself.

Open thoughts, free-writing, and the final party to thank you... but when are we going to have a ball?

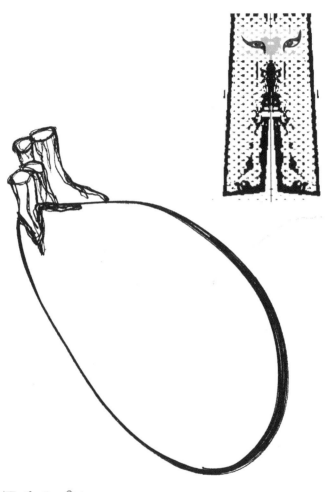

EGGPLANT HEART

■ "Catch" The Cure.

190

Music is an individual pursuit.

When sanity is too disturbing,
the sounds of madness reassure us.
Many songs ran through my grunge blood,
singing my teenage crush cuts.
The verses spread the bitterness of love,
hugging us all in a farewell to RIP.

2.22.22 shouldn't be written in history
as your last breath.
A strong voice that sang our lives
was silenced on the day of
The Death Of Romantic Love

"...and my love travels with you.
Whatever you are."

— — — -

Quando la sanità mentale è troppo inquietante,
I suoni della follia ci rassicurano.
Molte canzoni scorrevano attraverso il mio sangue grunge,
cantando i miei passionali tagli giovanili.
I versi, diffondendo la dolcezza dell'amore,
Si abbracciano in addio nel buio del loro silenzio.

22.2.22 non dovrebbe essere scritto nella tua storia,
come punto fermo.
Quella voce forte che ha cantato le nostre vite taceva il giorno della
"Morte dell'Amore Romantico".

"...and my love travels with you.
Whatever you are."

"I Was In Love With You" The Gutter Twins.

"Sworn and Broken" Screaming Trees .

"Come Undone" Mark Lanegan and Isobel Campbell .

"Beehive - Andrew Weatherall Remix" Mark Lanegan.

"Bleed All Over" Mark Lanegan.

"This Lullaby" Queen Of The Stone Age.

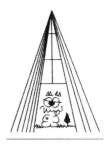

ARIGATO MONEY

"Ghost of Love" David Lynch

192

<u>My Yellow House is burning inside.</u>

My body is changing. Like time, everything is in motion while I gently press the clooney part of my hand, relaxing the headache. This projector has to wait for energy in order to run the machine.

Facts of life. I love my age but It's a shame that I haven't archived a more refined way to let the frustrations to go away. It includes my mistakes, limitations, and narrow views, which all will change as time goes by.

I appreciate all the help and advise, and I am especially grateful for all the fab songs given from another heart.
The music on my Spotify lists were feed by amazing minds who I really want to be always close. There is no money that can buy this transmissions of thoughts.

I'm still getting out of the red, some expected turbulences around my Kingdom, then my sofa is my lounge and my troubled daughter is very ill. Lilly is being brave; sometimes it is hard; a mother should never see her kid perishing.

Focusing else where, it's ringing for action under the sun!
A few parties to DJ, trips to unknown places, and a lot of laughs with amazing people. The path for "The Death of Romantic Love" project is transmuting into long-last new loves! To my partners in different crimes, my flag waves goodbye to unfinished business. Everybody hurts, anyway! Violet lights for all of us.
Everything is a circle echoing inside out.

My life is my own love letter.
Let's do it in style!

Thank you so much for your support.

Cheerio,
Patricia Regina Coppa Boreham
a.k.a. P.O.L.L.Y.

193

THE GATE TO LOVE

■ "All My Life" Foo Fighters.

DO NOT DISTURB CHILDREN
WHEN THEY ARE SKATEBOARDING.

THIS BOOK IS FULL OF GENETIC CODES, SECRETS AND
INFORMATION FROM OTHER COSMOS.

QUESTO LIBRO È PIENO DI CODICI GENETICI, SEGRETI E
INFORMAZIONI DI ALTRI MULTIVERSI.

この本は、遺伝暗号、秘密、および他の多言語からの情報で
いっぱいです。

CE LIVRE EST REMPLI DE CODES GÉNÉTIQUES, DE SECRETS ET
D'INFORMATIONS D'AUTRES MONDES

EAGLE EYE ON PITTA!

**CUTTING CORNERS; LISTENING TO THE SONG BELLOW
FRESH AS A DAISY, THEN YOU WOULDN'T RECOGNIZE ME.**

"The Truth" I Like Trains.

196

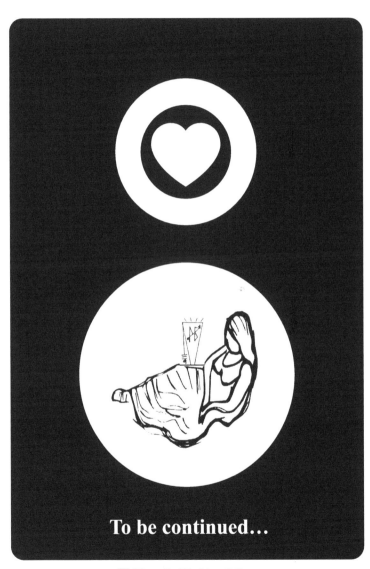

To be continued...

"I Love You" Fontaines D.C.

9999999999999999999999999999
9999999999999999999999999999

Printed in Poland
by Amazon Fulfillment
Poland Sp. z o.o., Wrocław
13 June 2022

b2c93b7d-25ae-493e-87d4-b9ab992282d6R01